365 Windows

Halford E. Luccock

ABINGDON PRESS
NEW YORK • NASHVILLE

365 WINDOWS

Copyright © 1955, 1956, 1957, 1958, 1960 by Halford E. Luccock

Library of Congress Catalog Card Number: 60-5232

SET UP, PRINTED, AND BOUND BY THE
PARTHENON PRESS, AT NASHVILLE,
TENNESSEE, UNITED STATES OF AMERICA

PREFACE

~~~~~~~~~~~~~~~~~~~~~~~~~~~~~~~~~~~~~~

There is a villa between Padua and
Ferrara in Italy which has three hundred and sixty-five
windows. That is plenty of windows for even a large house!
It has been conjectured that the original builder had in mind
the 365 days of the year when he installed as many windows
in that house, and that it was his intention to suggest that one
could look out, and *ought* to look out, upon the world each
day from a different window.

The hope that has led to this little volume is that it may
provide 365 windows for 365 days of the year. George Herbert
Palmer, wrote in an introduction to a volume of the poems of
George Herbert, that "most friends of the spirit speak from a
pocket volume." It is my hope that this volume may at least
speak a bit, and that the windows may look out on an
alluring landscape. May they prove to be awakeners and not
tranquilizers! The entry for each day will take only two minutes
to read, but it is hoped that the two minutes may sometimes
spread over a day. We often hear the command, "Stop a minute!" No one can really *stop* a minute, but one can do that
in a true and different sense. The influence of an arresting
moment of thought may be continued for a whole day and
longer.

5

I am grateful to the editors of *Christian Herald* in which magazine the enclosed devotions appeared originally for their kind permission to use them. Also my appreciation goes to Mrs. Carol Kelly for the delirious job of reading my handwriting and typing the book.

HALFORD E. LUCCOCK

CONTENTS

~~~~~~~~~~~~~~~~~~~~~~~~~~~~~~~~

7

A Christ Distance Away

Week 1—Day 1 ~~Sept. 10, 1965~~ **Read Mark 10:46-52**

There is a striking, arresting phrase in a poem by Edna St. Vincent Millay. The theme of the poem is, in general, sympathy with those in need. She speaks of seeing a starving begger and she "felt his gaze and heard his moan." She describes a tragedy as being "only a Christ distance away." That is a new way of measuring distance, "a Christ distance away." That means very close. Some people can look at suffering and be miles and miles away in their thought, even though it is only across the street. The proper distance from a person we know in need, or people we know in need, is just a "Christ distance away." That requires love.

Alert our minds, O God, that we may be near in our sympathy and response to those in need. Amen.

Week 1—Day 2 **Read I Cor. 6:19, 20**

The German Emperor, Frederick William I said, "Salvation is of God. Everything else is my affair." That has often been a common claim of kings. It is false. Everything in life and in the world is God's affair. Worship is God's affair, but so also is the whole of human life, its work, its play, its

11

wealth, its power. All is God's affair, and he should be made the master of all life.

Because, O God, we know that thou art both wise and good, we offer thee both what we are and what we have. Amen.

Week 1—Day 3   **Read Ps. 69:20**

J. B. Priestley made a true observation about our times in one of his novels. He said, "One thing the matter with our modern world is that too many people are leading lonely lives." He added that though they are living in cities and large towns and are constantly moving among crowds, they are desperately lonely. As Christians it is one of our responsibilities as well as privileges to befriend people constantly. This truth was put into an old gospel song. There must be many who still remember it, "There are lonely hearts to cherish, while the days are going by." Are there lonely folk to whom you could give heartening friendship?

O God, who settest the solitary in families, we pray for thy comfort to those who lead lonely lives. May we be thy messengers of friendship. Amen.

Week 1—Day 4   **Read Heb. 13:1-3**

One of the finest and truest definitions of sympathy is, "Sympathy is your pain in my heart." It is more than just a casual look at someone in trouble and saying, "Too bad. I'm sorry," and then dismissing it from our mind. That is too easy to be called "sympathy." When some other person's pain is really felt in our hearts, then we have sympathy we can call "Christian," because it is the kind of outgoing love which Christ showed.

Save us, O God, from getting so wrapped up in ourselves that we never feel any pain in anyone else. May we give of our care and help, not sparingly, but in full measure. Amen.

Week 1—Day 5   **Read Matt. 5:44-48**

George Bernard Shaw made a definition of a gentleman, which is well worth carrying in the memory. "A gentleman," he said, "is one who puts back a little more than he takes out." That reverses an idea of a "gentleman" which was common many years ago. In the eighteenth century in Europe a gentleman was considered to be a person of privilege and exclusiveness who lived by taking as much out of the common wealth as he could and putting back as little as possible. Today the ideal of life of many people is to get through life with as little trouble and labor as possible. This definition of Shaw's fits in with the word of Jesus, "Whoever would be great . . . must be your servant." Think how much we take out of life! Others have labored, and we have entered into their labors. How much do we put in?

Help us to give ourselves, O God, in personal relations with others, not grudgingly but in full measure, pressed down, shaken together, and running over. Amen.

Week 1—Day 6   **Read Phil. 2:2-5**

Some members of a college faculty were discussing the wife of a colleague. One man said, "That woman

13

is a seismograph! She can record a shock all the way from a boy falling from his bicycle across the street to an earthquake in Japan." That was a high tribute! A seismograph is an instrument for recording tremors and shocks of earthquakes. Each of us ought to be a seismograph in that sense. We ought to be in our community "the nerve o'er which creeps the else unfelt oppressions of the earth." Jesus was sensitive to the sights and sounds of human need. Are we?

God our Father, open our ears to music. Let us thrill to spring's first flutes and drums, but never let us dare forget the bitter ballads of the slums. Amen.

Week 1—Day 7   **Read Col. 3:9-13**

Miss Elizabeth Peabody, a pioneer in the kindergarten movement in America, started in Boston over a hundred years ago. She advertised that it would be a "very exclusive school." That very word "exclusive" suggest walls shutting out people. But her school was of a different kind. She said, "Snobbery and vulgarity are vigorously excluded." They were!

What kind of "exclusiveness" do we go in for? Do we draw lines against people of another class, race, or color? Or do we rigorously exclude snobbery and vulgarity from our lives?

O God, the Father of Our Lord Jesus Christ, and of all men, deliver us from every form of exclusiveness in relation to our brothers in Christ. Amen.

14

WEEK 2

Consider the Turtle

Week 2—Day 1   **Read Isa. 35:3-5**

It is recorded that when James B. Conant was president of Harvard University, he kept among other objects on his desk a little model of a turtle under which was the inscription, "Consider the turtle. He makes progress only when he sticks his neck out." That is true! You can prove it by watching any turtle. No turtle ever moves forward when he is enclosed within his shell. Will you consider the turtle today? How carefully we guard our necks! We become so afraid of taking any risks for a good cause! Our neck is *not* the most important thing about us. Our soul is the most important thing. We must take risks for God's church and for his kingdom.

Help us, O God, to seek first thy kingdom and to count all else but loss for the privilege of being fellow workers with Thee. Amen.

Week 2—Day 2   **Read Matt. 9:9-12**

There is a scene in King Lear in which the banished Duke of Kent returns disguised to the Duke of Albany's palace, seeking to serve the king again.

"What wouldst thou?" asks the king. "Service," replies the duke. "Who wouldst thou serve?" "You." "Dost know me, fel-

15

low?" "No," says the Duke, "but you have that in your countenance which I would fain call master."

There is in the countenance of Jesus that which we are constrained to call Master. If we look at him long enough, if we let him walk before our imagination, we will call him Master and ask with Paul on the Damascus road, "What wilt thou have me do?"

We thank Thee, O God, that Jesus does call us o'er the tumult of our life's wild restless sea. Help us to respond to his "Follow me." In his name. Amen.

Week 2—Day 3   Read Luke 5:3

There is a remarkable painting by the artist, Rode, entitled "Christ in the Class Room." It is a painting of a European schoolroom into which Christ has entered. The teacher has arisen and allowed the Master to take his place at the teacher's desk.

The painting is a powerful expression of a great idea, that of allowing Christ to use our occupation for his work and message, just as that teacher allowed Christ to use his classroom. Christ used Peter's boat. He can use our occupation.

Take our talents, O God, and use them for Thy purposes of love. In Jesus' name. Amen.

Week 2—Day 4   Read Luke 12:40

A woman sent this excuse for her son's being tardy, to the kindergarten teacher in a New York school. She wrote, "Please excuse Johnny's being late to school this morning. Nine o'clock came sooner than we expected!" Hardly a good excuse! So many things, including 9:00 o'clock, do often come sooner than we expect. The testing of our strength of character by temptation has a way of jumping on us suddenly when we do not expect it. It was so with Peter the night of Jesus' arrest. The test by the fire in the courtyard came sooner than he expected, and he failed in his loyalty to Jesus. Be ye therefore ready, for ye know not the hour.

Grant, O God, that day by day our spirits may keep awake and that we may watch and pray that we enter not into temptation. Amen.

Week 2—Day 5   Read I Cor. 15:57-58

We need encouragement quite often to keep us going through discouraging days. Here is one bit of history, showing how great things were accomplished by patient continuance. The average speed of the *"Mayflower"* during much of the voyage across the Atlantic to America was *two miles an hour!*

That was enough to discourage even the hardiest souls on that momentous journey. Two miles an hour! That voyage was a glorious example of pushing on under discouragement. It is a good thing to remember when our speed toward some cherished goal seems to be two miles an hour!

Help us, O God, not to be weary in well doing, knowing that with thy help, we shall reap if we faint not. For Jesus' sake. Amen.

17

When Lady Mary Wortley Montague, the witty letter writer and society figure of the eighteenth century, came to the end of her life, her last words were, "It has all been very interesting." It is good to have an interesting life, of course. But not as an ideal of life, as though we were only spectators of the drama of the world with no responsibility for service, no obligation of duty, but just looking to be entertained.

Contrast that idea of life with the one pictured in the last word of Jesus, "It is finished." Jesus came to do the will of God, and he had done that will. It was finished. He came "not to be ministered unto, but to minister." How about us?

Save us, O God, from living our lives carelessly and selfishly. Amen.

Many years ago a young woman named Anne Walter Fearn went to China as a medical missionary. Her mother was terribly anxious about Anne's safety on the trip out to China. She gave the girl a twenty-dollar gold piece with which to send back one word by cable on her landing, the word *"safe."* The young missionary spent the money for a cablegram, but she did not send the word "safe." She sent another one-word cable: "Delighted." The word "delighted" is far more jubilant and a far more Christian word than "safe." Some folks never in their lives get beyond the word "safe." There is no exuberance in their discipleship, no risk in their living for Christ. Jesus offers something better: "Enter into the joy of the Lord." Be delighted in him, and the chance to serve him.

May we enter into the joy of our Lord who did not bid us to live safely, but to take up our cross and follow him. Amen.

Out of This World

Week 3—Day 1   **Read Ps. 91:1-4**

A very true and fitting tribute to the power of the Christian faith is this, that it takes a person out of this world and puts a person into it! That is not only a striking arrangement of words, designed to get attention by its strangeness, but it is also completely true. Christian faith *does* take us out of this world. It takes us out of time into eternity, into the mind and heart of God. It is a tragedy to be "earth bound," to have no power in life which lifts us out of our darkness, sorrow, and night into the wonderful joy of the light of God in the face of Jesus Christ.

Our Christian faith also *puts into the world* in a new and deeper manner. In Christian living we do not draw away from the world with its great need, but, fortified by communion with the God who is "out of this world," we go into life to minister to its need in Christ's name.

May we respond to thy great invitation, "Come unto me," that having received of thyself, we may go into all the world to share with our fellows what thou hast given us. Amen.

Week 3—Day 2   **Read John 15:11-14**

The British novelist, Charlotte Brontë, was once given the advice, dispensed by a terribly solemn person with little imagination, to "grow happiness." She exploded! She said vigorously, "Happiness is not a potato!" Surely it is not! Happiness does not come to people as a farmer grows potatoes. True happiness comes from earnest and generous living. Disciplined living defeats the destructive forces which would make true happiness impossible. And happiness comes from unselfish living. "He that loseth his life shall find it."

May we find the joy of the Lord in his service. Amen.

Week 3—Day 3   Read I John 4:16-21

Greenfield Village is the name of the New England town created by Henry Ford in Dearborn, Michigan, by bringing together from many places houses connected with American history. The advertising slogan used is "Where American history comes alive." Let that suggest to us another phrase, "Where the gospel history comes alive." Where would that be? The answer is clear. The gospel history comes alive— not in a physical place but in a spirit. Wherever the spirit of sacrificial love is expressed in a life, there the gospel "comes alive."

We thank thee, God, for the gift of thy love. May it come alive in our spirit and deeds. Amen.

Week 3—Day 4   Read I Thess. 1:3-7

Some time ago a man had a flat tire on his way to church on Sunday morning. He arrived at the church very late. As he was hurrying up to the church door, he met another man coming out. He inquired, "Is it all done?" The man coming out of the church gave an unexpected answer. "No," he said, "it has only been *said*. We are just starting out to *do* it." It is not enough to say and hear noble things. We must *do* them.

Help us, O God, to make evident by our lives that our religion is not in word only, but in deed. Amen.

Week 3—Day 5   **Read John 13:3-4**

Think carefully of the different kinds of service to a man and to God which we can render by the work of our hands. A preacher wrote about this many years ago. He puts these words in the mouth of a faithful woman, "God takes a hand whenever he can find it. Sometimes he takes a bishop's hand and lays it on a child's head in benediction; then he takes the hands of a doctor to relieve pain, the hand of a mother to guide her child, and sometimes he takes the hand of an old creature like me to comfort a neighbor."

Take our hands and let them move at the impulse of thy love. Amen.

Week 3—Day 6   **Read Jas. 2:15-16**

A man once wrote, "The test of a vocation is the love of the drudgery it requires." Think it over. The word "love" in that connection seems pretty strong, but it fits a vocation. The doctor, for instance, has to do untold drudgery, but very, very often the physician so loves his high vocation of ministering to health and life. The same is true of a nurse and of a mother.

We cannot say that we really love a form of service unless we endure without complaint the drudgery that makes it possible. We must love serving men and women so that for the joy of it we are willing to do the drudgery without which the service is impossible.

May we, O God, with thy help, walk without fainting. Strengthen us for endurance in hard tasks for thy love. Amen.

Week 3—Day 7   **Read John 9:4**

A preacher announced to his congregation that he was going to preach on the twenty-ninth chapter of Acts. Some heads nodded gravely to indicate that they knew what was in that wonderful chapter. Then the preacher told them that there was no twenty-ninth chapter of Acts; there are only twenty-eight chapters! But, he said Christianity is a continued story. Each generation and each person adds new chapters to the story. We are the twenty-ninth chapter of The Acts of the Apostles. We are to add to the stories the acts which we perform as apostles of today.

We thank thee, O God, our Father, for all who have labored and into whose labors we have entered. May our own labors add to the story of The Acts of Apostles. Amen.

WEEK 4

An Unfavorable Balance of Trade

Week 4—Day 1   **Read Ps. 103:1-5**

How do your irritations compare with your enthusiasms? Some people get into the habit of allowing their irritations at other people, and at things and events, to become their chief response to life. Others see and enjoy the positive good, and their enthusiasms displace gripes and complaints. When your irritations are more and greater than your enthusiasms, you have an "unfavorable balance of trade."

Give us, O God, the grace of enthusiasm about the best things of life. May thy gifts never be taken for granted, and may our thanksgivings drown all complaints and murmurings. Amen.

Week 4—Day 2   **Read Jas. 3: 5-8**

Here is a noble prayer of Phillips Brooks: "O God, give me the strength to live another day. Keep me from losing faith in people. Keep me sweet and sound, in spite of occasional ingratitude and meanness. Above all, keep me from giving little stings, and minding them. In the name of the Strong Deliverer, Jesus Christ. Amen."

Look well at the words, "Keep me from giving little stings." We all know that temptation. We think that some word is a bright remark, and it may be. But its unkindness is more

24

notable than its wit, and it causes pain like the cutting of a knife.

Set a watch on my lips, O God, that my words may carry sympathy and love and not stings of any kind. Amen.

Week 4—Day 3   **Read Mark 8:34-37**

The autobiography of publisher George H. Doran records a conversation between Andrew Carnegie and Frank N. Doubleday, another publisher. Carnegie asked Doubleday how much profit he made in a month. Doubleday answered that the publishing business could not be figured in that on-the-spot fashion. "Then," said Carnegie, "get out of it, Frank, get out of it."

That is a typical attitude of people who want to show an immediate cash profit on all that they do. Whatever does not show a profit, they regard as a failure. We all need to watch and pray that such a commercial measurement of life does not become the measure we adopt.

Help us to measure life, not by money, but by service to people in need and by walking humbly with our God. In Jesus' name. Amen.

Week 4—Day 4   **Read Rom. 14:12**

"No one of us has a blank in the pages of the Recording Angel." That sentence written by George Bernard Shaw brings close home to us our responsibility to God for our actions. None of us escapes from that responsibility. Our God is a God of love, but he is not a God of indifference to evil. We are writing a page each day.

We pray earnestly, O God, that we may write on life's pages, by thy help, records which represent our best endeavor. In Jesus' name. Amen.

Week 4—Day 5   **Read Matt. 27:27-30**

There is one detail of the scourging of Jesus by the Roman soldiers before his trial which ought to cause us deep personal concern. We read, "and [they] put a reed in his right hand." (Matt. 27:29) That was a crowning mockery. They gave him a mockery of a king's scepter. They gave him a weak reed with no power at all. Let us hold that picture in our minds and think of ourselves. Do we give to Jesus only the semblance of power over our lives but no *real* power? Give him a scepter!

O God, may Jesus Christ take his power and reign in our lives. In his name. Amen.

Week 4—Day 6   **Read Rom. 15:13-14**

Edmund Leamy has written some lovely verses, expressing wonder that a ticket agent in a travel bureau can sell tickets to the wonderful places of the earth and have no more emotion about them than if they were five pounds of potatoes! He writes:

26

"Like any merchant in a store

. . . .

He deals with scarce perfunctory glance
Small pass-keys to the world's Romance." [1]

Does that description of routine indifference fit us sometimes?
In our faith we have "pass-keys" to the greatest romance in the
world, the sublime story of the love of God in Christ. Do we
feel it deeply enough or do we just take it for granted?

*Help us, O God, from day to day, not to take thy love and
care for granted, but to feel the wonder of it, and to respond to
thee in joyful obedience. Amen.*

[1] From "The Ticket Agent," used by permission of Harper's Magazine.

Week 4—Day 7   **Read Luke 17:13-15**

In her fascinating book *Gift from the Sea*
Anne Morrow Lindbergh makes a plea for the preservation of
the inner spiritual life and for the renewal of the inner life
of the soul. Among other things that ought to be cast off she
writes of the duty of "shedding" things that crowd out the
soul. Among other things that ought to be cast off she
mentions "the shell of ambition, the shell of material accumula-
tions, the shell of one's ego . . . one's pride, one's false ambi-
tions, one's mask." Look at your own life. Is there anything
that you might "shed" to the benefit of the soul?

*Help us, O God, to pluck out from our lives whatever spoils
us and chokes the good seed within our souls. Amen.*

27

I'm Sitting on Top of the World

Week 5—Day 1   **Read I Cor. 9:25-27**

An old song, "I'm Sitting on Top of the World," has been sung by many people who were not "on top of the world." *The world was on top of them.* A New York newspaper recorded the fact that on a New Year's Eve a man was taken to the police station, drunk and disorderly, singing this song at the top of his voice. It was not very convincing!

We are really "on top of the world" when we are on top of the forces which might draw us down: our appetites, our greed, our hatreds, our anxieties, our fears. It is God whose power and love make us masters of our circumstances. As Paul wrote, I keep my body *under.*

May we receive, O God, the strength for living which thou dost desire to give us. In Jesus' name. Amen.

Week 5—Day 2   **Read II Pet. 3:17-18**

A railroad in the East has petitioned the state to be allowed to eliminate "telltales" before bridges or tunnels. The "telltales" are strips of lightweight materials hanging over tracks to warn men riding on top of the cars of bridge or tunnel ahead.

In our lives how much we need "telltales" to warn us of

dangers to our character! We need reminders of dangerous temptations at hand. John Wesley's mother gave to him a "telltale" about amusement. She said to avoid whatever dulled the edge of the appetite for spiritual things.

In the hour of trial, Jesus, plead for us. May we be alert to the danger of betraying thee in our conduct. Amen.

Week 5—Day 3   Read II Cor. 5:17-19

Some months ago the newspapers carried the story of Sol A. Stephen who was superintendent and later general manager of the Cincinnati zoo for a period of sixty-seven years. Think of the excitement of managing a zoo for all that time! Yet each of us has a job something like that, for we have traits within us that resemble some animals. We tend to be vain like peacocks. Sometimes we are like stupid geese. Sometimes we hurt people as do fierce animals. Tennyson has a line about us. "Let the ape and tiger die." We must allow the love of God to subdue our evil powers.

We thank thee, O God, that if any man is in Christ he is a new creature. May thy spirit rule our spirits. Amen.

Week 5—Day 4   Read I Cor. 15:51-58

One of the sad sights of the tropics is that of Europeans who have "gone native." That phrase means dropping the customs, the clothing, and the ways of thinking and living of the home country and adopting the ways of life of the country to which they go. This degeneration frequently starts with a delighted acceptance of the wealth of earth, sea, and sky. It is followed by an easy relaxation of the usual controls, physical and moral. As the man's linen loses starch, his convictions also become limp.

One does not need to go to the tropics to lose one's moral and religious standards. One can "let go" anywhere!

In the hour of trial, Jesus plead for me lest by base denial, I depart from thee. Amen.

Week 5—Day 5   **Read II Pet. 1:5-8**

A puzzled man exclaimed in perplexity, "Life is a lot like a kid's problems in arithmetic. We add when we ought to subtract, and we get all mixed up." Many of the serious mistakes in life are really mistakes in arithmetic. Men in frantic pursuit of wealth keep on adding and multiplying goods when they ought to be dividing their wealth among institutions which bless mankind. All of us are tempted to subtract from the list of people we care about when we ought to add to the list. Or we often add to the number of our selfish gratifications when we ought to substract from them, for the sake of self-discipline and service.

How do you handle these arithmetic problems?

Help us, our Heavenly Father, to add to our faith virtue, and to virtue, knowledge, and to knowledge temperance, and to temperance patience. Amen.

A man was standing on the deck of a large ocean liner, the "Queen Mary." Looking at the prow of the ship cutting the waves, he asked a sailor how far the ship would have to go before it could stop if it were going at full speed. "Well," answered the sailor, "she couldn't even slow down in less than a mile. It would take more than that to stop. You see, with a big ship like the "Queen Mary," *you have to think a mile ahead.*" Two days later when the ship was making her way through busy, crowded New York harbor, it was very evident that the pilot was "thinking a mile ahead."

In life we should think miles ahead. Most of the tragedies and failures of life have come from "spot thinking." That is, just considering the immediate with no thought for the future. The heavy drinker does not think a mile ahead to see a ruined life. He thinks only of immediate gratification. The man who drops religion and the church out of his life does no mile-ahead thinking. He does not visualize the years "when age comes on uncheered by faith and hope."

Thou hast shown us, O God, in Jesus Christ, the things that make for life and death. Help us to choose life. Amen.

In one edition of the story, *Gulliver's Travels,* published many years ago, there was a drawing that some readers may possibly remember. Gulliver had landed on a strange, fanciful island, Lilliput, which was inhabited by very small people no larger than his thumb. He was overcome with exhaustion and fell asleep on the beach. The little people who discovered him asleep were afraid of such a monstrous giant and tied him to the earth by hundreds of little strings. Gulliver, when he awoke, was still a giant, but he was helpless, tied by little strings.

It can be a disturbing picture. It may be a picture of the life of any one of us. For many times we are held back from undertakings in which we ought to engage by little strings; that is, by things which are not important in themselves, but which do tie us down and spoil our best possibilities. A student, for instance, may fail to achieve success because he is "tied down" by many little time-wasting engagements. People are often kept back from being the force they might be in the Church of Christ, because they are kept back by such little strings as, "I can't go to church. It is four long blocks." (The man who said that walked two miles around a golf course the day before!) Or one may say, "I work hard for six days; I need to sleep till noon on Sunday." Have you any little strings?

Save us, O God, from a small self-concern which keeps us from sharing the great adventure of being workers together with thee. Amen.

WEEK 6

Casting Problems

Week 6—Day 1   **Read John 12:24-26**

Here is an announcement which often appears in statements concerning forthcoming plays: "Casting problems are holding up production!" That means that the play is all written, all ready, but the difficulty is to find actors who are capable of playing it.

Shakespeare's *Hamlet* is all ready, but it is hard to find an actor to play the difficult role. Transfer that whole situation to the Christian enterprise. The script is all written. It is presented clearly in the New Testament. What the world needs, what God needs, is a company of people who can play the parts in God's drama of the evangelization of the world. Are we part of the problem of finding a cast?

Lord, speak to us that we may speak in living echoes of thy tone. Amen.

Week 6—Day 2   **Read Isa. 44:21-23**

A woman complaining about her typewriter said that she wanted to return it because there was no key for an exclamation point. "My letters are full of exclamation points," she said. "How can I write if I have no key for one?" (A typist could tell her, all right!) But, so often, the lack of an exclamation point affects more than a typewriter. Many people have no exclamation points in their minds and hearts. They have nothing about which they go all out in joy and gladness, so life is poor. They plod along in a critical mood, complaining, and with no high joy in life. The grace of God brings joy into life. Isaiah wrote, "Break forth into singing." Jesus said, "These thing have I spoken unto you, . . . that your joy might be full." Don't lose your exclamation point!

May the God of hope fill us with all joy in believing. Amen.

Week 6—Day 3   **Read Luke 13:22-24**

Think today of one word as it occurs in the New Testament, the word *strive*. It is a very active verb. It does not suggest an afternoon nap or lazy folding of the hands. In Luke 13:24 we read: "Strive to enter in at the straight gate." That does not mean "saunter in." In Rom. 15:30 we find Paul's earnest request: "Strive together with me in your prayers to God for me." Prayer calls for striving! All through the New Testament discipleship is pictured, not as a carefree stroll through life, but as a *fight* with evil, a *striving*. Can our concern for moral and religious effort be truly called *striving*?

Help us, O God, to fight the good fight with all evil powers and strive to win mastery over them. Amen.

Week 6—Day 4   **Read I Tim. 4:10**

A very influential church leader was speaking to a company of people on some of the dangers of old age.

Among other things, he said, "I notice in myself that as the years advance, I have a very strong tendency to think that the easy way to do anything is the right way." Check yourself on that point. Concluding that the easy way is the right way is not a mark of old age exclusively. It can happen in middle age and youth, for it is an attractive thing to choose the easy way. It is easy to "do as others do," but it is hard to say (and live up to it), "We must obey God rather than man."

Grant, O God, that we may be given the force of mind and heart to seek always to do the right thing and not the easy thing. Amen.

Week 6—Day 5   **Read I Cor. 15:28**

Hold two things together in your mind. One is a sentence from Moffatt's translation of the New Testament. "We are a colony of Heaven." To that beautiful picture add a chapter of early American history. That chapter is the story of the famous "lost colony." Sir Walter Raleigh brought a company of colonists to North Carolina. A few years later, when a ship came back across the Atlantic, no trace of the colony was found and none has ever been found. Christians ought to be a "colony of heaven," a company who acknowledges the rule of God and seeks to spread the kingdom of heaven. But they can become a lost colony, bearing no allegiance to God and his kingdom.

Keep our minds and hearts alert, O God, that we may keep our discipleship. Amen.

One of the most "deadly" words in the language—a word which has been a great obstacle to religious and social progress—is the word "average." It is a word which brings a false satisfaction, in that it makes people satisfied with low standards. Some people are complacent about their giving, for they say, "I'm giving as much as the average," forgetting that the "average" includes children. The word "average" can be a tyranny. It leaves no place for distinguished character and action.

Jesus did not call his disciples to "average" discipleship, or to be satisfied with a lazy, casual following. He said, "Be ye . . . perfect, even as your Father which is in heaven is perfect."

Help us to remember, O God, that not failure but low aim is crime. Amen.

In a play written a few years before the outbreak of World War II, in the days when Hitler's barbaric tyranny threw terror into the nations, there was a memorable line. One character, thinking of the threats to the world, said, "They are taking the world away from the intellectuals and giving it to the apes." One listener said, "If that is true at all, perhaps one reason is that the 'intellectuals' do not fight as hard as the 'apes.' "

That is sometimes true. Often the people who believe in

democracy do not work as hard for it as some Communists work for their own vicious way of life. Think it over. How hard do we work and fight for the Christian faith?

Help us, O God, to fight the good fight with all our might, that thy truth may prevail. Amen.

The Only Local Thing

Week 7—Day 1   **Read I Pet. 5:6-8**

One of the rewarding and sustaining things about the Christian faith is that it is *personal*. The Gospel comes to us as individuals, as well as to the whole world. This means much in a world and in a time when so much of our life lacks any personal touch. A wise man, Archie Robertson, said this about his life in a small town: "The church is almost the only local thing that is left, except the Virginia Creeper. Most people ride the Greyhound. The schools have consolidated. The bread is baked 50 miles away. We get our thought from New York and Washington. Everything is canned."

In our gospel, everything is not canned. The gospel is still gloriously personal. It calls for "casting all your care upon him, for he careth for you."

May our faith not be a formal affair, but a personal receiving of thy truth, and a personal dedication to thy work. Amen.

Week 7—Day 2   **Read John 1:11-13**

Consider this question, "How do you think of yourself?" This does not mean, "Do you think too much of yourself or too little?" though that question is important. It means, "Just what do you think you are?" Someone has written,

"It is what we think of ourselves that, in the long run, determines the conduct of men and of nations." If we think of ourselves as just mechanical accidents or a higher grade of animals, life loses its high meaning. But if we think of ourselves as sons of God, the objects of his love and care, then that makes all the difference in the world and in eternity.

May we keep in our minds, O God, the wonder of the love the Father hath given us that we should be called the children of God. Amen.

Week 7—Day 3   Read Luke 15:4-7

We all remember the letters made familiar in World War II—V.I.P. They meant "very important person." Those given the rating of V.I.P. were given priorities on airplanes and other special attention. From the standpoint of Christian faith every man is a V.I.P. to God. Every person has an infinite and individual value to God and an eternal place in his love. That is a tremendous thing to believe, but we have a tremendous gospel. The high meaning of the parables of the lost sheep, the lost coin, the lost boy, is that one person is immeasurably important to God.

Lift our minds and hearts, O God, up to the high faith that God loves us as individuals. May we always treat every person well, remembering that he is a very important person to thee. Amen.

You have often heard the phrase, "dull as ditchwater." A person who is bored says of a situation or happening that it is "as dull as ditchwater," as though that were the dullest thing in the world. But someone pointed out that ditchwater, so far from being dull, was one of the most exciting things on earth to one who could really see. For, of course, ditchwater is full of squirming life, full of bacteria, which have an enormous importance for our lives.

When we complain that people or places are dull, it usually means that *we* are too dull to see.

Open our eyes, O God, that we may behold wondrous things out of thy Word, and wondrous things in thy world. Amen.

It is rewarding to go through the Gospel and note how many times it is recorded that Jesus looked at a person. Thus in Luke 19:5 Jesus looked on Zacchaeus. In Luke 22:11, Jesus turned and looked at Peter. But there was more to it than that. There must have been something special about the way Jesus looked at people. For one thing, we know that he *really saw them!* Do we look at people carefully enough to see their needs, their desires, their possibilities? Such a look would impel us to act.

Open our eyes that we may see not only beautiful things around us, but also that we may see the needs of people, and be swift to help where we can. Amen.

Sometimes a casual word from a person who is a complete "outsider" to the meaning of the Christian gospel throws a shaft of light on its high meaning. No one could have a firmer claim to the title of "a complete outsider" to the Christian gospel than Napoleon Bonaparte, arch brigand and mass slaughterer. He wrote, after the battle of Bautzen, "I lost no one of importance." He lost thousands of soldiers in that battle, but "no one of importance!" That is just what our gospel does not say! *Every* child of God is of infinite importance! Here is our glorious gospel—in the mind and heart of God there is no one not important!

We thank thee, O God, for the assurance that though men and women may be "last" in the opinion of the world, in thy love the last shall be first. Amen.

One of the strangest things in the history of Christianity has been the fact that many of the finest tributes to the Christian gospel and faith have come from enemies. One of the first written attacks on the Christian church was by the Roman writer, Celsus, who in the latter part of the second century made a slashing attack in his book, *True Discourse*. He tried to cover the faith with ridicule. All he succeeded in doing was to cover it with glory! He wrote thus, in condemnation, "The root of Christianity is its excessive valuation of the human soul and the absurd idea that God takes an interest in man." Also he wrote, in scorn, "Everyone who is a sinner, who is devoid of understanding, who is a child, whoever is unfortunate, him will the Kingdom of God receive." Thank God for "the absured idea that God takes an interest in man"! It is the glory of our gospel!

We thank thee, O God, that what seems foolishness to many is the power of God and the wisdom of God. Amen.

What Do You Lack?

Week 8—Day 1   **Read Mark 10:21-22**

Consider the cry of street vendors away back in Athens, Greece, long before the Christian era, and also in London in the eighteenth century. Socrates heard the tradesmen cry as they went along the street—"What do you lack?" and in the eighteenth century along London streets the cry, "What do you lack?" was familiar. Ask yourself this old question—"What do you lack?" Is there anything missing which life needs—the peace of God which passeth understanding, or the strength which comes from him who strengthens us?

Teach us, O God, to ask largely that our joy may be full. Amen.

Week 8—Day 2   **Read Luke 15:8-19**

The woman who found the lost coin in Jesus' parable cried out, "Rejoice with me." That means, literally, "Congratulate me!" How often we use words of congratulation. And frequently in what trivial connection, over a new dress, an automobile, a new decoration of some kind, an increase of salary! At other times the words mark a real red-letter day—the coming of life's great gifts and trusts, marriage, the birth of a child, or some significant toil and achievement.

The words here as Jesus uses them in the parable of the lost coin picture life's deepest and most lasting cause for congratulation, that we have become part of the forces for good of the world. Beside that, congratulations on many other scores are like the chatter of a child's tea party.

Lead us, O God, into the deepest and most lasting sources of rejoicing, that we have become part of the force of thy love in the world. Amen.

Week 8—Day 3   **Read Prov. 22:1; Mark 8: 34-37**

What are the things in life which represent to us the summit of success? A student of American life described recently what he said was the ambition of many suburbanites. They strive, he said, to be like the "upper-middle class." They are convinced that the proper mixture of golf, cocktail parties, membership in the right clubs, and the proper amount of expenditure, represent the last plateau to which they are striving. Do you have any "plateau" of life higher than that? In that connection consider the question Jesus asks in our scripture reference today.

Grant, O God, that no distractions of material success and prestige may draw us away from seeking first the kingdom of God and his righteousness. Amen.

Week 8—Day 4   **Read I Cor. 4:9-13**

Consider this remark of Robert Louis Stevenson, "Give me the young man who has brains enough to be a fool." On the face of this that sounds foolish and can be very foolish. It doesn't take much brains to be a fool in the sense frequently used. One kind of a fool is pictured in the words, "A fool and his money are soon parted." The foolish person who ruins his life by dissipation is a sad sight.

Stevenson did not mean that kind of person. He meant a man who, for the sake of a great result, did things that selfish, conventional peope call "foolish." Such a person is a man who "throws his life away," as they say, like a missionary who prefers spiritual integrity to wealth.

Help us, O God, to make the hard choices for service to others, rather than gain for self. Amen.

Week 8—Day 5   **Read Gal. 6:9-10**

There is a phrase often used, "the shut-ins," meaning those who are compelled by sickness or injury to stay in the house, "shut in" from the busy life of men. But there are others who make shut-ins of themselves. They shut themselves away from taking part in efforts to improve conditions in the world and in the church and community. They cannot be counted on to do an adult share of work in a good cause. They are "shut-ins" too. There is a needed ministry of the church to those self-made "shut-ins." It is to say, "The Son of God goes forth to war, who follows in his train?"

Break down our excuses for self-indulgence, O God, and send us forth to labor for thee. In Jesus' name. Amen.

A radio announcer in Hartford, Conn., used to finish a broadcast with the words, "This is your friend and mine, Bob Steele." It is a turn of words which is ingenious. Then follows the mental agreement, "Of course, a person is naturally a good friend of himself." But is it necessarily true that we are always good friends to ourselves? We can be enemies of ourselves. We are enemies of ourselves when we do not put our appetites under discipline. We are not good friends when we fail to keep ourselves up to our best.

Grant us wisdom, O God, that we may seek earnestly to make the best of our possibilities. Amen.

In a prayer meeting not long ago the congregation sang vigorously the old gospel song, "On Christ, the Solid Rock, I Stand." They made the rafters ring with the music. When they had finished, a thoughtful layman arose and said, "I have enjoyed singing that song with you. But I think it needs something else to go with it. For we ought to do more than *stand* on Christ. We ought to stand *with* him in the battle against all forms of evil today, against injustice, discrimination, cruelty and war." Think that over. Do we stand *with* our Master when the battle is on?

O God, we have promised to serve thee to the end. Give us grace to follow our Master and our Friend. Amen.

WEEK 9

The Forgotten Key

Week 9—Day 1   **Read Heb. 3:5-6**

In *Pilgrim's Progress* John Bunyan recounts a tense incident which happened to Christian. It might be called "The Forgotten Key." Here is a part of it in Bunyan's words, "Now, a little before it was day good Christian, one half amazed, brake out in passionate speech, 'What a fool' quoth he, 'am I, thus to lie in a stinking dungeon, when I may as well walk at liberty! I have a key in my bosom called promise, that will, I am persuaded, open any lock in Doubting Castle.' . . . Then Christian pulled it out of his bosom, and began to try it on the dungeon door, whose bolt gave back, and the door flew open with ease, and Christian and Hopeful came out with ease."

This is a very true picture of experience. God's promises will bring deliverance in hard situations if we will trust in them and act on them.

We thank thee, O God, for the great and precious promises of thy word. Help thou our unbelief. May we have a larger and more active trust in thee. Amen.

Week 9—Day 2   **Read Prov. 23:17-19**

There is an arresting idea in the scripture listed for reading today. Proverbs 23:17 reads, "Let not thine heart envy . . . but be thou in the fear of the Lord." This is an inevitable alternative. If a person has no high sanctities, he will have low superiorities. The only bulwark against the destructiveness of envy is a greater concern with reverence which lifts our life to a higher level. We can take our choice.

We thank thee for revelation of thyself, O God. Keep us in the spirit of reverence for thee and thy commands. Amen.

Week 9—Day 3   Read I Cor. 15:19-23

At the funeral service for the poet, Robert Browning, one of those attending was Browning's great friend, the painter, Edmund Burne-Jones. Afterwards, Burne-Jones said that the service was far too somber to express the glory that was in the life of Browning. He said, "I would have given something for a banner or two, and much would I have given if a chorister had come out from the triforium, and rent the air with a trumpet." That is a good phrase to think of when our minds turn to the end of life, for our friends or ourselves. It is not, as the hymn wrongly asserts, "death's cold sullen stream." The death of a Christian is a time for the blowing of trumpets, for the triumph in him who has brought life and immortality to light.

O God, we give our grateful and heartfelt thanks for our Master who could not be held by death. Take away from us, we pray, all fear of the future, knowing that whether we live or die, we are the Lord's. Amen.

In these days of hurrying here and there, of rushing about this and that, the average person tends to be more and more cut off from the past. There is a word for it from the French, *deracine*. Few people in our large cities know where their great-grandparents are buried, or even who they were. This goes deeper than the lack of lasting physical roots. It applies, all too often, to our minds. They can become cut off from the past, from all the great events that have happened in the past. The past, such as God's revelation to Israel, the life and teachings of Jesus, the noble works of saints and prophets, apostles and martyrs may be cut off as a force for present living.

May we keep our minds freshly aware of the great past of our faith and hope. Amen.

One of life's blunders is to try to get from *things* the satisfactions for the spirit which can come only from spiritual sources. The British novelist, J. B. Priestley, has put this truth briefly and forcibly. It comes to our day with special force, for we are in a gadget-minded time: "We cannot get grace from gadgets. In the bakelite house of the future, the dishes may not break, but the heart can. Even a man with ten shower baths may find life flat, stale and unprofitable." Jesus put this same truth in other words when he condemned the man in the parable of the rich fool, for having many things but not being "rich toward God."

Unto thee, O God, do we lift up our hearts. Thou hast made us for thyself. May we never seek our satisfactions in things less than thee. Amen.

Week 9—Day 6   **Read Luke 4:18-21**

We are all familiar with the edict of the White Queen in *Alice in Wonderland*—"Jam yesterday and jam tomorrow, but never jam today." We may smile at that, but many people go through life on that schedule. Something good may have happened yesterday; something good may happen tomorrow. But nothing good ever happens today! So the whine goes. For them today seems to be an empty place between yesterday and tomorrow.

Note in our scripture reading for this date that the first recorded word of Jesus' ministry was the word *today*. He said, "Today this scripture has been fulfilled in your hearing." (R.S.V.) The promises of God are good *today*. The joy of the Lord is obtainable *today*. God's power is available, not only yesterday in history, and tomorrow in eternity, but *today*.

Save us from being too busy to dedicate ourselves to thee today, and to ask largely of thy grace, that we may be equipped for Christian living, not tomorrow, but today. Amen.

Week 9—Day 7   **Read II Sam. 18:32-33**

We hear much in these days about our living in a new world. But the most important things in life are the *old things*. A minister thought of that while making a pastoral call. He was sent for by a man whose son had just died. The minister talked on the telephone. That was new. He drove to where his friend lived in an automobile. That was new. He went into a sixteen-story apartment. That was new. He went up in an elevator. That was new. Then he faced a father in his grief. That was not new. That was old. It was as old as a room above a gate in Jerusalem, where a father, King David, cried out, "O my son Absalom, my son, my son Absalom! would God I had died for thee!" The biggest things in life are not new inventions but old reliances of faith.

From everlasting to everlasting, thou art God. Amen.

Casually Yours

Week 10—Day 1   **Read Phil. 1:9-11**

A manufacturer of women's coats advertised a coat named "Casually Yours." The advertisement said that "it catches the air of informal unconcern."

These phrases arrest our attention and lead us to think, not of coats, but of people in relation to the church and to the kingdom of God. Is it not a danger for any of us, that we, like some others, have "an air of informal unconcern" for the church, and our relation to God becomes "casually yours." For people who come to church only occasionally and who put God's work way down on their list of priorities, their relation to God is "casually yours." Nothing less is adequate than to be to God, "*tremendously* yours"!

May we love thee, O God, with all our strength, soul, and mind. In Jesus' name. Amen.

Week 10—Day 2   **Read Col. 3:1-4**

One of the memorable books of World War II is the record of a British prisoner of the Japanese, entitled, *Officially Dead*. This British officer was kept in solitary confinement. He describes the exploits he carried on to keep from losing his mind, dredging his mind for every piece of information he had ever learned, every poem, every song, every piece of learning. He won his battle for preserving his sanity.

Somewhat like that, we have to struggle to keep a Christian mind, amid so many pressures to dull the edge of our Christian commitment. If we give up the struggle, the sharp religious quality of mind is gone.

Help us, O God, having done all, to be obedient to thee, to stand. Amen.

Week 10—Day 3   **Read II Cor. 4:16-18**

In a novel by Galsworthy entitled *The Saint's Progress,* one person laments the fact that the bells of the church, while still beautiful, are out of tune with the "music of the streets."

That ought not to be a cause for sadness but for gladness. For the Christian church does not take its tune from what is popular on the streets, but from the eternal word of God. The young church in Rome was "out of tune" with the prevailing customs and ideas of Rome, but it was in tune with the infinite God.

Help us, O God, to be in accord, not with the fashions of men but with the will of God. Amen.

Week 10—Day 4   **Read Matt. 13:1-8**

We have all heard, over and over again, the saying so much used by the Russian Communists that "religion is the opiate of the people." The idea that Communists try to spread abroad is that religion lulls people into a sleep. Some people have used religion in that perverse way. Multitudes of others have found in religion an "awakener" to action. There is an "opiate" which has affected many people, however. It is a danger to each of us. It is *pre-occupation*. We can get so busy with our minds and hearts filled with many minor concerns, that we never give to God and our religious faith and obligations the attention they deserve.

May we, O God, leave room in our lives for the greatest matters. Amen.

Week 10—Day 5   **Read John 3:1-5**

There is a challenging sentence in a poem which Edward Arlington Robinson wrote about Nicodemus, who came to Jesus at night. The poet pictures Nicodemus going to the high priest, Caiaphas, and telling him of the new insights and experiences which had come from his talks with Jesus. "There is no life in these old laws of ours," Nicodemus says. "They are forms and rules and fears." But Caiaphas replied, "I know you, Nicodemus. You will not stand up for this prophet, Jesus, when he is under attack."

That is a disturbing comment. Will we stand up in broad daylight and support Jesus when it is costly or dangerous?

Save us, we pray, O God, from shameful retreat when we should stand firm.

Hold your mind for a few moments on the verse, "bringing into captivity every thought to the obedience of Christ." It is a beautiful picture of a devotion to Christ so strong that it ties life together like a stout binding cord. A lady drifting down the river in a boat fell asleep, and the string of pearls around her neck became unfastened, and one by one the pearls fell into the water. That suggests a life which comes to pieces. When our days are not strung on a strong cord of one purpose, our life becomes a collection of unstrung pearls. Saving life from this calamity is to have devotion to God as the cord that binds our days together to achieve a unified life.

Help us, O God, to string our days together along thy purpose for us. Amen.

A woman who had been in an accident was in a traffic court explaining how she drove her car. She said to the policeman who had arrested her, "I always drive with the emergency brake on so that when there is an emergency, I will be ready. That, she thought, was being on the safe side!

There are many people who seem to go into any kind of service to other people with the emergency brake on! They are good at holding back. They never let themselves go with any self-forgetful abandon. Take off the emergency brake!

Help us, O God, to forget our own selfish interests, and whatever our hands find to do, to do it with all our might. Amen.

WEEK 11

High Altitude Lethargy

Week 11—Day 1   **Read Gal. 6:8-10**

The leader of the mountain climbing expedition which conquered Mount Everest was speaking about some difficulties of the climb. He stressed the importance of "training the will so that it can drive the body after the 'high altitude lethargy' sets in."

Tuck the phrase away in your mind, "high altitude lethargy." Evidently, when climbers get up at a high altitude, weariness and sleepiness set in. Also in personal life there can be a "high altitude lethargy." Weariness may set in when we reach a high level of religious living. We need the power of God, daily renewed, to sustain it.

Will thou fortify us with thy presence, O God, that we may not be weary in well doing, but may walk and not faint. In Jesus' name. Amen.

Week 11—Day 2   **Read I John 1:6-7**

There is a wise counsel for the spiritual life in the words of a poet, Stephen Spender, swear:

"Never to allow gradually the traffic to
            smother

56

With noise and fog the flowering
of the spirit." [1]

These are two things which are enemies of "the life of God in the soul of man"—noise and fog. We live amid clanging noises. We must make a place of quiet for the soul to "be still, and know that I am God." Also, to avoid fog, we need to keep in communion with the Light of the world, so that the guiding light of God's truth may be clear.

Grant, O God, that we may walk in the light as Christ is in the light. Amen.

[1] "I Think Continually of Those Who Were Truly Great," Random House, Inc., 1938, 1946.

Week 11—Day 3   **Read Rev. 21:5-7**

A recent book, popular among the many collectors of antique furniture, glassware, and jewelry, is entitled, *How to Restore Antiques*. Evidently, the restoration of antique furniture, particularly, is quite an art.

There are "antiques" in the life of the spirit. There are precious possessions in the religious life, things which have come down from God's revelation in the Scriptures and in the experience of people. Among the precious legacies from olden times are trust, the sense of God's presence, the assurance of his forgiveness, fellowship with him in worship and service. These need to be continually restored. They must be brought freshly to mind, and put into practice.

May we, O God, be restored by the renewing of our minds, and may thy great gifts be made new. In Jesus' name. Amen.

One of the greatest physicians of our century, Sir William Osler, once gave some good advice on how to end the day. He wrote, "At night, as I lay aside my clothes, I undress my soul, too, and lay aside its sin. In the presence of God I lie down to rest, and to awaken a free man, with a new life." A wonderful way to end the day. Osler's suggestion echoes the words of the hymn, "Now the Day Is Over," thus:

> When the morning wakens,
>   Then may I arise
> Pure, and fresh, and sinless
>   In Thy holy eyes.

We commit ourselves to thee and to the doing of thy will, every evening and morning. Amen.

Following the story of the healing of the lame man at the gate of the temple, it is recorded that "the man was above forty years old, on whom this miracle . . . was shewed." Surely there is a valid suggestiveness in this fact, a picture of God's grace to those in middle life. God does shew "miracles" to people above forty years of age. In the middle years people do need God's grace for there are besetting dangers, the danger of forgetting the early dedication of life to God, the danger of increasing tasks and increasing wealth, causing a slackness of religious life. For all these real needs, his grace is sufficient for us, if we will ask.

Save us, O God, from every distraction that wasteth at noonday. In Jesus' name.

Week 11—Day 6   **Read Rev. 3:1-5**

A French writer once said to young people, "Lay up for yourselves a good many enthusiasms in your youth, for you will lose many of them along the way."

That is true. We do lose enthusiasms as we grow older. Some enthusiasms we ought to lose; these are the "childish things" which we put away. (I Cor. 13:11) We ought to lose our enthusiasm for rattles or bubble gum. Tragedy comes into life when we lose our enthusiasms for the finest things in life. We do not need to lose them. It is an immeasurable loss when we lose our enthusiasm for worship and the church, for active working for the human welfare, for reading good books, because without such enthusiasms, the life of the spirit dies.

Grant, O God, that we may never outlive our love of thee. Amen.

Week 11—Day 7   **Read Isa. 40:29-31**

A visitor once came upon the noted modern musician Pablo Casals practicing very slow scales upon the cello. "But, master," the visitor said, "surely you don't need to practice scales!" The musician replied, "Ah, my boy, the whole problem in playing the cello is how to get from one note to the next." That is the big problem, isn't it—how to get from one day to the next? How to come through the days without loss of faithfulness, without weariness that might bring disloyalty to our commitment to God's work—that is a lifelong concern and for that concern God promises the renewal of the mind. Read about it in Rom. 12:2.

May we not in our own strength confide, O God, for then our striving will be losing. May we follow our leader with renewed strength day after day. Amen.

WEEK 12

Singing Out the Hours

Week 12—Day 1   **Read Ps. 103:1-5**

A newspaper report from Spain recorded that in the Spanish town of Ciudad Real, the ancient custom of "singing the hours" has been revived. Using tunes that date back to the Middle Ages, watchmen go through the streets, singing information about the time and weather.

It is a suggestive thing to think of, "singing the hours." Most of us would not add to the enjoyment of our neighbors by singing out the time every hour! But we can go through the day with a song in the heart, "singing out the hours" by a song of thanksgiving in our hearts and minds, a song of dedication to God. Thus the day becomes not a listless trudge but a walk with God.

Will thou waken, O God, our hearts, hour by hour, that we may not forget all thy benefits. In Jesus' name. Amen.

Week 12—Day 2   **Read Ps. 118:24**

Some people get into the bad habit of failing to enjoy and appreciate the present time because their eyes are fixed on the future when there will be, they think, more to appreciate. That cripples life greatly. We read in Proverbs that "the eyes of a fool are in the ends of the earth." Also, the eyes of a fool are often fixed on tomorrow, and so he forgets the possible joys of today. It was said of a poet, "She was one of the few who were able to appreciate that wonderful pleasure, the present, and her letters are radiant with immediacy."

Today is the day to receive and enjoy God's gifts, the beauties of nature, the joy of trust in God, the blessings of home and friends, the chance of service to others.

We pray, O God, not for scenes more wonderful, but for eyes to see the wonder of thy gifts that we already have. Amen.

Week 12—Day 3   **Read Ps. 63:1-7**

An advertisement for electrical fixtures gave this advice, "Have your living room flooded with interior light."

A good thing for a living room! And a good thing for a life! It is a very good description of Christian experience. If faith and trust in God are in our hearts, our whole being may be flooded with "interior light," no matter how dark and gloomy the outward scene. "Yea, though I walk through the valley of the shadow of death, I will fear no evil." For our whole mind and spirit will be flooded with the light of joy that comes from the spirit of God in our lives.

Because thy loving kindness is better than life, O Lord, may our lips praise thee, and our lives obey thee and show forth thy goodness. Amen.

Week 12—Day 4   **Read Ps. 37:3-6**

In the first verse of the third chapter of Philippians Paul writes, "Delight yourselves in the Lord! It

62

doesn't bore me to repeat a piece of advice like this." This is in the translation by J. B. Phillips. Let those words sink into our minds . . . "It doesn't bore me." So many things do bore so many people. Their work bores them, doing the same thing over and over. Even their friends bore them. Sometimes their church bores them. They allow it to become a routine, mechanical thing.

It did not bore Paul to say a good word for the Lord or to do a good deed for him. It ought not to bore us. It will not if we keep alive the recognition of God's gifts to us. Freely we have received. If we remember that, it will not bore us to give.

Help us, O God, to delight ourselves in the Lord, and to enter into the joy of serving him. In Jesus' name. Amen.

Week 12—Day 5   **Read Isa. 55:12-13**

In G. B. Shaw's gripping play *Major Barbara,* the mother of a young woman who has joined the Salvation Army says to her in disgust, "Good gracious, Barbara, you talk as though religion was a pleasant subject." There are people, including many professed Christians, who act as if religion were an unpleasant subject—a sort of necessity to be put aside as soon as possible.

But the religion of Jesus Christ is the most pleasant subject in the world. Uncounted millions of people have found it so. Jesus said, "These things have I spoken unto you, that my joy might remain in you." Do you get all the joy from your faith that you might?

May we live our lives and do thy work, O God, with the joy which belongs to those who are fellow workers with thee.

Week 12—Day 6   **Read Mark 10:46-50**

The poet Thomas Gray, of England, many years ago wrote this acute observation: "In Cambridge there is nothing so troublesome as that one has nothing to trouble one." The poet lived a quiet life with no disturbances, nothing to trouble him. He found it hard to endure. For, having no trouble, with nothing to worry about, comes pretty close to being dead! Jesus wished that our joy might be full. So he said, "Take up your cross and follow me." In other words, pick up a load of trouble. Carry some burdens for the welfare of others. Thus you will be kept alive. You will belong to the greatest fraternal order on earth, the friends of the human race.

Keep us out of easy places, O God, and out of selfish removing of ourselves from the needs of others. Amen.

Week 12—Day 7   **Read Matt. 9:36-38**

An advertisement of a steamship line not long ago, quoted part of a letter received by the company from a woman passenger. It read, "That was the best gift I have ever had—a trip into wonderful country." That could be, if the "country" were not Greenland or the Sahara Desert.

A fine gift. But in a true sense, there is an even better gift and a more wonderful country. It is the gift we may all have, the gift of following Christ into the most wonderful "country" on earth, a journey into other lives, into the needs of other peoples, where people sit in darkness and hunger and cold. That is real adventure.

May we, O God, in our thinking and living, bear the invitation of him who said, "Come unto me all ye that labor and are heavy laden." Amen.

Begin the Day with Music

Week 13—Day 1   **Read Mark 1:32-35**

"Begin the day with music." These words often appear in advertisements of radios, especially those with built-in alarm clocks. The clock can be set for a certain time in the morning, and the sleeper will be awakened by music from the radio. It is a good idea—to begin the day with music of another sort. Begin with the music of a thankful heart, the response of heart and mind to God's gift of a new day. Jesus began the day with dedication, "I come to do Thy will." That spirit in us will keep life from being a drudge and make it a walk with God.

Waken our spirits we pray thee, day by day. Help us to receive each day as a fresh gift from thy hands, and strengthen us for the duties that lie before us. Amen.

Week 13—Day 2   **Read Ps. 107:1-6**

Think over this observation on human nature: "A man's discontent is due not to what he has or lacks, but to what he sees others enjoying, while he goes without." Is that not true, at least, very often? Against that envy which destroys inner peace, there is no sure defense except a spirit of thanksgiving to God. If we have gratitude for what we have, and think of that, we will overcome discontent. The Swiss theologian, Emil Brunner, has well compared thankfulness to swimming. He writes, "So long as there is air in the lungs, we do not sink. So long as we cherish thankfulness to God in our hearts, the heavy load will not bear us down. Hence, let us be careful to see that air remains in our lungs, and gratitude does not melt away."

Grant unto us, thy children, O God, a consciousness of thy indwelling presence, so that we may have utter confidence in thee. Amen.

Week 13—Day 3   Read Ps. 104:1-6

A real and costly calamity in the life of anyone is to get into the habit of taking things for granted without any sense of fresh wonder or remembrance of the Creator of the world. In *A Victorian Boyhood*, L. E. Jones comments on this danger: "Children have a disappointing habit of taking the wonders of the world for granted, and of grumbling, like elderly clubmen, about the food and the plumbing."

Do we go through life like "elderly clubmen" complaining about things? Think twice before you answer! How different Jesus was with the glad appreciation of the lilies of the field! Keep alive your sense of wonder over all of God's gifts.

O God, who hast given us all things richly to enjoy, may we never take thy bounty for granted, but may we see the world about us with amazement and give thanks with heartiness. Amen.

Consider a picture of thousands of lives, whose exploits are never celebrated in newspapers, but whose names are written in the most important "Who's Who"—the Lamb's Book of Life. This picture is found in the words of George Eliot, "The growing good of the world is partly dependent on unknown acts. That things are not so ill with you and me as they might be, is half owing to the number of people who lived faithfully a hidden life, and rest in unvisited tombs." Recall the blessings which have come to you from lives "hidden" from the crowd but known to God. With gratitude, may we determine to join the company whose hidden lives are the blessing of the world.

We praise thee, O God, for all those who have touched our lives with blessed helpfulness. May we pass on to others love and help like that which we have received. Amen.

Here is one of the hazards of living, the danger of being so absorbed in the gifts of life that we forget the great giver, God. This is pointed out by John Ruskin thus: "Dependence on God is forgotten because bread is given and the water sure. Gratitude to God may cease because his constancy in protection has taken the semblance of natural law. When God is forgotten, the heavenly hope may grow faint, amidst the full functioning of the world."

Keep in our minds, O God, the remembrance that all things come from thee. Give us the grace of thanksgiving. Amen.

When Herman Morse was elected moderator of the Presbyterian Church, U.S.A., he made a speech modestly saying that any recognition that had come to him was due to the services of others. Then he said, to enforce his point, that when you see a turtle on a stump, you know he did not get there all by himself! The same is true of each of us. We may not have arrived at the very top of the stump, but wherever we are, we did not get there all by ourselves! We have entered into the labors of others. That calls for humility and gratitude and in turn our service to others.

Save us, O God, from complacency and self-satisfaction and conceit. Deepen within us a sense of what we owe to others, and help us make a fitting response to that debt. Amen.

Someone once asked General A. W. Greely, the distinguished army officer and Arctic explorer, what he considered his greatest achievement. He replied, "Bringing up six children on an army officer's pay." Multitudes of parents will agree with him! There must be a special reward in heaven for those who bring up a family of fine children on a limited income, often severely limited! That surely is one of life's greatest achievements, for it is an undertaking which counts enormously in the world's welfare. Consider the family of Timothy in our scripture reading for today. He was the first third-generation Christian of whom we have any record. He was an evidence that the church would go on. That was a shining achievement of his mother Eunice and his grandmother Lois.

Accept our thanks, O God, for all the gifts which have been passed on to us by loving parents. Put thy blessing on all fathers and mothers, and give them thy grace and guidance. Amen.

WEEK 14

Innocent Bystander

Week 14—Day 1   **Read Obad. 1:11-12**

We often hear the phrase "innocent by-stander." Sometimes a bystander is completely innocent, as when one is forced to watch a street accident in which he has had no part. But often our claim to be "innocent bystanders" has little foundation. When an act of cruelty is done in our midst and we make no protest, we are not "innocent." Our keeping still makes us condone the wrong. When we show the emotions of prejudice and ill will, and that prejudice bursts out into violent actions, ours is part of the blame. If we have not worked for peace, we are not completely innocent of the evils of war if war comes through neglect in which we have had a part.

We pray thee earnestly, O God, that in all conflict with evil we may not stand aside, but may come boldly to the help of the Lord against the mighty. Amen.

Week 14—Day 2   **Read I Cor. 9:24-27**

A cartoon a few months ago showed a pathetic gentleman at the optician's to be fitted for glasses. He says, "I'd like to see things a little less clearly, please." We smile at that, but it has a real point that all of us can feel in these troubled days. There are times when we feel that we would like to see some of the evils of the world and threats to the world "a little less clearly, please." But as Christians it is our duty to see the evils of the world clearly. We should use our eye to detect the opposition to God's will in the world so that we shall be able to be fellow workers with him, to overcome evil with God.

Anoint our eyes, O God, that we may be clearsighted fighters for thee and may not beat the air. Amen.

Week 14—Day 3   **Read Rom. 12:1**

              In a story a detective examining a house where a robbery had been committed, said, "This was almost a perfect crime. The man did not leave a single print anywhere."

Think that over. Is it not the perfect crime in life not to leave your fingerprint on anything? Think of a person going through life and not leaving a personal touch on some task that needs to be done, or some person on whom we might have left a fingerprint of personal influence for good. Have you left your fingerprints of personal interest and service anywhere?

Into thy hands, O God, we commit our lives this day. Whatever our hand finds to do, may we do it for thy sake. In the spirit of Jesus. Amen.

Week 14—Day 4   **Read Mark 10:46-50**

              Here is an effective picture of exclusiveness as achieved by a woman who made a lifelong practice of it,

Mrs. Potter Palmer of Chicago, the acknowledged "leader" of Chicago "society" in the late years of the nineteenth century. Her house was a vast treasure house of art, more like a warehouse than a residence. In it she was the undisputed queen of hostesses. To reach her presence, the visitor's card had to pass through the hands of twenty-seven butlers, maids, and social secretaries. Even her closest friends were obliged to write for appointments. This raises a smile, but it also raises a serious question—"Do I live behind walls of exclusion, or am I accessible to human need or loneliness, as Jesus was accessible to those who called out to him from the roadside?"

O lead me, Lord, that I may lead, the wandering and the wavering feet; O feed me, Lord, that I may feed the hungering ones with manna sweet. Amen.

Week 14—Day 5   **Read Mark 4:23-24**

Jesus never gave any lessons on how to speak. He talked much on how to *hear*. He said, "Take heed how you hear." So many of us today live in a bath of noise. The really important things in the world to hear are the still, small voice of God, and the still, sad music of humanity. Neither makes a resounding din. We have to listen carefully to the voice of God in our hearts and the sad music of people in need.

Grant unto us, O God, sensitiveness of spirit, that we may hear thee speaking to us, and grant us the dedication that we may do thy will. Amen.

A truly Christian art is the art of putting ourselves in the place of another so that we may know where life's burdens bear heavily on him. A man who mastered this art in a wonderful way was John Woolman, the Quaker. He wrote about what he practiced, "It is good for those who live in fullness to practice every opportunity of being acquainted with the hardships and fatigues of those who labor for their living, and thus to think seriously with themselves, Am I influenced by true charity in fixing all my demands?" Do we pay little attention to the miseries of others, as long as they are not before our eyes?

May we keep our eyes alert and our minds sympathetic that we may not pass by on the other side of human need. Amen.

One of the great achievements of Christian faith and discipleship is to love people. Not just "nice" people, "our" kind of people, but all kinds of people. It is easy to say, "I don't like people." That makes it easy to "let the rest of the world go by." Edward Lear, the humorist, did this. He said, "I grow so tired of new people, and silly people, and tiresome people, and fanatical people, and robustious people, and ugly people and fussy people—and people altogether."

We cannot say that, or anything like it, and fulfill God's command, "Love one another."

For the sake of him who loved us and gave himself for us, O God, help us to show love to all kinds of people. Amen.

WEEK 15

Undelivered Tidings

Week 15—Day 1   **Read I Cor. 9:16-18**

        William Watson, the English poet, has a couple of lines about a poet which should cause us all to do some heart searching. He writes: "The undelivered tidings in his breast suffered him not to rest." Ask yourself, do you have any sense of "undelivered tidings" in your breast? The good news of Christ was meant for all. It has reached you. Has it ended with you? Have you tried to deliver the good tidings to anyone who has never really received it?

For the good news of the gospel, O God, which has come to us we lift our hearts in gratitude. Help us to share the tidings of thy love. In Christ's name. Amen.

Week 15—Day 2   **Read I Cor. 3:13-16**

        Martin Luther laid great stress on the truth that work is religious, too. We are accustomed to call work "secular" and worship "religious." Luther tried to correct that false idea. He wrote: "What you do in the house is worth as much as if you did it up in heaven before the Lord our God. It looks like a small thing when a maid cooks and cleans, and does other housework, but because God's command is there, even such a lowly employment must be praised as a service to God." The same truth is in George Herbert's hymn:

"Who sweeps a room, as for
the Lord,
Makes that and the action
fine."

*Help us, O God, to praise thee in the skill and devotion
with which we do our daily work, and may all our work be a
reflection of the spirit of Jesus, who said, "I must work the
works of him that sent me." Amen.*

Week 15—Day 3   **Read Matt. 5:14-16**

It is an old story, but it is true, and it is
good. The famous British author John Ruskin, one night in his
later years, sat watching a lamplighter who, with a torch in his
hand, was lighting the lamps on a distant hill. The man himself
could not be seen, but the lights would gleam as each one was
lighted. Ruskin said to a friend, "That is what I mean by a real
Christian. You can trace his course by the lights he leaves
burning."

*Give us strength to show forth thy goodness, O God, not
for our own gratification, but that others may see our good
works and glorify our Father who is in heaven. Amen.*

Week 15—Day 4   **Read Rom. 12:10-13**

Here is one man's picture of a friend, a
well-known federal judge: "He is possessed of that zest of life
which precipitates joyfulness in others. He has a gift of im-

mediate intimacy, and a flattering memory for past encounters. When he comes into a room many agree that it is as if all the lights had suddenly been switched on, and a match put to the logs on the hearth." Think of that. Isn't that tribute a finer thing than to say, "He was worth a million dollars"? Is it candlelighting time when we come around, or do people look for the nearest exit? As disciples of him who is the Light of the World, we should be light-bringers.

Give us, O our Father, faith strong enough for any darkness, and may we be the bringers of joy to those among whom we move. Amen.

Week 15—Day 5   Read John 21:15-17

Let us look at three strong words and then look at ourselves. Emil Ludwig, who has written many biographies of men of different sorts, including Napoleon, Bismark, Goethe, and even Jesus, said some memorable things about writing biography. He said, "If you are to write a biography of a man, you must think with him and eat with him. You cannot make a person live in the mind of another unless you have a furious, mad, passionate relationship to him." We have been commissioned to make Christ live in the minds of people. Would anyone suppose that we had a "furious, and passionate" relationship to Christ?

Were the whole realm of nature mine, that were a present far too small. Love so amazing, so divine, demands my soul, my life, my all. Amen.

A young man once went to Charles H. Spurgeon, the world-famous preacher, in London, told him that he had had to call to preach, and asked Spurgeon what he should do. Spurgeon looked at him with great affection, but asked him an embarrassing question, "Can you preach?" The young man said, modestly, "I suppose I wouldn't set the Thames on fire." "No," said Mr. Spurgeon, "I suppose not. But if I threw you in, would you make it fizz?"

A good question for each of us. None of us will set the Hudson River on fire, or the Mississippi or the Colorado. But if God throws us into any community, as he has done, will we make it fizz? Will we make an emphatic witness for Christ that can be noticed?

Help us to offer ourselves to Thee, our time, our strength, everything great or small. Amen.

About a generation or more ago when the Northfield Student Conference was attended by students from many colleges, the delegation from West Point was having a discussion of some campus problems. From a dark corner of the tent came a question from a student, "What is Christianity, anyway?" After a long silence came the answer from another corner, "Christianity? Why Christianity is Oscar Westover." The absent cadet to whom his mates bore such an impressive witness was the supreme argument. Christianity, to be powerful, must be incarnated in a life. What greater tribute could be paid to any of us, than to have it said, "Christianity is—our name"?

May our light shine, O God, not that it may bring us notice or praise, but that others, seeing in us the qualities of Christ, may be drawn to him. Amen.

WEEK 16

Anoint the Elbow

Week 16—Day 1   **Read Eph. 6:10-11**

Take hold of your elbow and then read this. The ordination of a king used to be, centuries ago, quite a thorough affair. When Charles II was crowned, not only was he anointed on the head, but also on the palms of his hands, on his breast, and on each elbow.

A good idea, anointing the elbow! For the elbow is the symbol of action. We speak of "elbow grease" when we have in mind power to get a thing done. That is what many of us need. Our minds and hearts are on the right side. We say of a person that "his heart is in the right place." But the elbow has never really been "anointed," that is, it does not act vigorously in God's service. There is need for anointed elbows!

Help us, O God, that whatever our hands find to do in thy service, we may do it with all our might. Amen.

Week 16—Day 2   **Read Rom. 15:1**

Joseph Conrad, the novelist of the sea, wrote frequently of what he called "the shadow line." By that he meant the line that divides youthful irresponsibility from adult responsibility. Some people never cross that line no matter how many years they add to their lives. They could repeat the line of poetry, "And still I am a child, though I grow old." How about us? Have we crossed "the line"? Have we taken responsibility gladly, instead of shrinking back? The kingdom of God moves forward on the feet of those willing to shoulder responsibility.

Make us dependable servants in thy kingdom, that having grown up, we may put away childish irresponsibility. Amen.

Week 16—Day 3　　　　　　Read Heb. 11:39-40

Someone once said truly, "It is a poor tribute to our forefathers to camp where they fell." Yet that is what some people often do. Each generation should go beyond the preceding generation in Christian enterprise. We have great tasks to do beyond the noble achievements of our forefathers. The evangelization of the whole world is our unachieved task. So is the task of making a more Christian way of life in the political and industrial and social world.

We thank thee, O God, for the vision and labor of those who have gone before us in thy calling. May we continue their work and go beyond what has been already done. Amen.

Week 16—Day 4　　　　　　Read Matt. 9:19-22

An impressive modern painting is one by Raymond Breinin, a painting with Christ as the central figure, entitled, "He Walks Alone." There is a landscape in blue, gray, and brown, showing a part of a city, with a group of figures on the right side, and on the left side the solitary figure of Christ walking on a bridge. The lonely figure of Jesus takes hold of the imagination. Jesus does walk in our cities. Does he walk alone, as far as we are concerned? Jesus walks among the sinful, among the needy folks, among the suffering. God wants us to walk with Jesus, helping his ministry.

O Master, let me walk with thee in lowly paths of service free. Amen.

Week 16—Day 5   **Read Acts 18:8-10**

In Shaw's play *Saint Joan* there is an impressive statement of the truth that true religion is not just an easy-chair affair, but calls for risk and danger. Before the sentence is passed on Joan of Arc, Bishop Cauchin says to Joan, "My child, you are in love with religion." Joan answers, "I never thought of that. Is there any harm in it?" The Bishop answers, "No, my child. There is no harm in it. But there is danger."

So there is danger in genuine religion. Danger that our life will be upset, danger that a faithful witness will cost us something. We are not called to go on a picnic but to take up a cross.

Give us the courage, O God, to pay the price of speaking and acting boldly in thy service. Amen.

The poet Robert Frost writes of the desire for reform, "it is a lovers' quarrel with the world." By that he meant that we should quarrel with the world and strive to make it better, not because we hate it but because we *love* it. We seek a better world. We seek to eliminate evil from our country because we love it. We seek to make our church a better instrument for God's use and not because we like to criticize all the time. In all our efforts for reform, our love must be strongly evident. We must guard ourselves lest we become so outraged by evil that we begin to hate the world.

May we remember that God loved the world, so that all our efforts at reform may come from love. Amen.

A man was looking over a large advertising booklet which came in the mail. Titled "Gifts for Casual Living," it listed with illustrations several hundred gadgets, most of them completely useless, supposed to be a held to "casual living." He decided there was already too much "casual living" —too much irresponsible, don't-care-much, "casual living" and not enough dedicated, serious living.

Here are some gifts for dedicated living: eyes that can see God's revelation in Christ, and also see needy people; ears that can hear the "still, sad music of humanity;" hands that can be laid on tasks of the kingdom of God.

Take our lives and let them be consecrated, Lord, to Thee. Amen.

WEEK 17

A Constant Flow of Vitality

Week 17—Day 1   **Read Jas. 2:15-17**

Here is one man's answer to the question, "What keeps Christianity going?" A Spanish scholar writes of culture in general: "Culture only survives when it receives a constant flow of vitality from those who practice it." Think of those words, "flow of vitality from those who practice it." Christianity survives, not from those who talk about it, but from those who actually practice it. Do we furnish demonstrations of what Christianity actually is in deed?

Grant, O God, that we may remember that our gospel is not in word only, but also in deed. So may others, seeing our good works, glorify our Father who is in heaven. In Jesus' name. Amen.

Week 17—Day 2   **Read Rom. 8:9**

A British statesman, Disraeli, a long time ago packed a great deal of wisdom—and of true religion—into a sentence. It is, "Life is too short to be little." Can you remember that? And act on it?

Think what a waste of precious days and weeks and years people have made in being "little"! To waste our short and precious time in "getting even," or saying nasty, cutting things, or being snobbish toward those who have fewer advantages than we, or to be grudging of our friensdhip and help, that is a tragically poor use of life.

We thank Thee, O God, for the gift of Christ, who has shown us the way. Save us from the long littleness of life. For Jesus' sake. Amen.

Week 17—Day 3   **Read Matt. 10:28**

Rudyard Kipling, poet and story writer, and William Booth, founder of the Salvation Army, had honorary degrees conferred on them the same day by Oxford University. William Booth was not embarrassed by the famous Kipling. He strode across to him and asked, "Young fellow, how's your soul?" Booth asked the "number one question." Beside that question, all distinctions of fame and wealth are as nothing. Ask yourself quite often, "How's your soul?"

Help us, O God, to put first things first in our lives. May the great prizes to be attained be the achievements in the spirit which make for likeness to Christ. In his name. Amen.

Week 17—Day 4   **Read John 8:31-32**

This sentence appeared over the desk of a newspaper editor: "Don't confuse me with facts. I've made up my mind."

The editor was joking, but he did state truly the attitude of many people. They have made up their minds, and they will not look at the facts which would lead them to reconsider their opinions. They condemn a whole group, or class, or people of a certain religion or color, refusing to look at the array of facts which demolish their prejudice.

There is a better attitude, stated in these words, "Ye shall know the truth, and the truth shall make you free."

Keep, we pray thee, our Father, our minds for the diligent search for truth. Amen.

Week 17—Day 5   Read Prov. 31:25-28

A book published a few years ago had this aluring title. *Decorate Your Home for Better Living.* Many would say on reading the title, "That is just what I want—better living." But on opening the book you discover that it is not about the *home* at all; it is about the *house!* The great mistake many people make is to confuse the house with the home. It is possible to have a luxurious house and a miserable home. The author of Proverbs put it vividly, "Better is a dinner of herbs where love is, than a stalled ox and hatred therewith." To decorate a home for better living calls for spiritual furnishings, kindness, alertness to feel what other persons really want and need, self-sacrifice, spiritual fellowship. Have we decorated our home with these?

Teach us anew, O God, that life is more than meat and the body than raiment, and that the inner life, filled with thy spirit, is more than any outward show. Amen.

          Consider the phrase in the Bible reading for today, "the sin that doth so easily beset us." Emphasize the word, *"us."* What are the particular sins that beset *us*? Many of us feel no temptation to commit the familiar gross sins of dissipation, such as liquor drinking, or gluttony. We are not tempted to steal or commit murder. Are we then free from sin? Hardly! Remember how sternly Jesus denounced sins of the disposition. They *do* beset us. Here are some sins that threaten us, self-righteousness, complacency and self-satisfaction, all kinds of snobbery, harshness in judging others, setting a higher value on observances than on kindness.

Help us to order our steps aright, so that we may walk with thee, O Christ. Amen.

          One of the most vivid pictures ever drawn of the devastating power of self-centeredness is the description which Charles Dickens gives of Dombey, the chief figure in the novel *Dombey and Son*. Here is Dickens' marvelous pen portrait: "Dombey and Son . . . those three words conveyed the one idea of Mr. Dombey's life. The earth was made for Dombey and Son to trade in, and the sun and the moon were made to give light. Rivers and seas were formed to float their ships, rainbows to give them promise of fair weather, winds to blow for or against their enterprises, and planets circled in their orbits to preserve inviolate a system of which they were the center. A.D. had no concern with *anno Domini*, but stood for Anno Dombey and Son." Read that and then ask the old, searching question, "Lord, is it I?"

We make our prayer unto thee, O God, that as the days and years go by, we may decrease and thou mayest increase in our lives. May our frantic self-insistence be overcome by the desire to know and to do thy will. Amen.

The World's Slow Stain

Week 18—Day 1   **Read I Cor. 10:13**

In a tribute to another poet Matthew Arnold wrote, "From the contagion of the world's slow stain, he is secure." Isn't that the perfect description of the way in which evil usually overtakes us, "the world's slow stain"? We do not, as a rule, go down before some dramatic temptation with a sudden crash. Evil comes as a "slow stain." It may even not be noticed. There is a gradual lowering of our standards; evil does not shock us so much; we get used to it. The slow stain is at work. "Keep thy heart with all diligence" (Prov. 4:23).

We thank thee, O God, for the assurance that thou wilt guide us with thine eye. Help us to be in the world as followers of Jesus Christ our Lord. Amen.

Week 18—Day 2   **Read Phil. 3:20-21**

One of the most interesting places in America to visit is the museum at Plymouth, Massachusetts. Among the many relics of earlier days preserved there are many pieces brought over in the "Mayflower." It stirs a mood of pathos, as well as admiration for their indomitable courage, to see these things which were brought from England. One thing is clear—the Pilgrims did not come over to Plymouth to "go native" in the wilderness. They were citizens of England and that high ciitzenship was never forgotten.

There is much temptation to us to "go native" in our surroundings, that is, "just do what everyone else does. Don't bother about any peculiar standards." But God said, "you are a peculiar people."

Save us, O God, from losing through carelessness the definite Christian quality of our lives. Amen.

Week 18—Day 3   Read Ps. 119:114-117

Sometimes it is interesting and arresting to come across a plea for Christian convictions made by one who makes no pretense of being a Christian believer. Here, for instance, are the impassioned words of George Bernard Shaw, pleading for "increased control of himself." That is what God's grace and love and power give to the individual. Mr. Shaw wrote in the preface to his play, *Caesar and Cleopatra*, "Of what avail are great machines, if the men who mind them are mean? Man's increased command of nature is paltry if it be not accompanied by an increased control of himself. That is the only sort of command relevant to the evolution of man into a higher being."

Help us, O God, to remember that saving of the world comes not by might, nor by power, but by thy spirit. Grant us thy spirit in our hearts that we may gain self-control. Amen.

Here is what Anne Morrow Lindbergh wrote of her need of a central "core" in her life, in her book *Gift from the Sea*: "I want to carry out my obligation to man and the world as a woman, as an artist, and as a citizen. But I want, first of all, in fact, an end to all these other desires, to be at peace with myself. I want a singleness of eye, a purity of intention, a central core to my life that will enable me to carry out these obligations." That is what we all need, isn't it? And here is a good core, our scripture for today, "bringing into captivity every thought to the obedience of Christ."

Give us a united heart, O God, that all our faculties and desires may be brought to the service of thy purposes for us. Amen.

Can you remember in the days of World War II the posters picturing the four freedoms? They were freedom to worship, freedom of speech and of assembly, and freedom from want. The phrase in our scripture verses today, in which Paul calls himself an "ambassador in bonds" suggests that there are noble bondages as well as noble freedoms. We are all called to be "ambassadors in bonds." We should have four great and ennobling bondages laid upon our lives. We should be in bondage to the *past*, that is, to have a commitment to carry on our great spiritual heritages from the past. We should be in bondage to the *future*, to work for a more Christlike world. We should be in bondage to *those in need*. We should be in bondage to *Christ* as Paul was proud to call himself the "slave" of Jesus Christ.

O God, the Father of our Lord Jesus Christ, who came not to be ministered to but to minister, take into thy hands our will to power and fashion it into the will to serve. Amen.

Week 18—Day 6   **Read Matt. 18:11-14**

Traveling Londoners left 122,000 gloves in London's buses and subways last year. Forgotten umbrellas were at a total of 62,000. There were 14,000 lost spectacles. We can understand how any person might lose an umbrella; in fact, you probably have mislaid an umbrella yourself! But many other articles were lost. But how many more valuable and precious things can be lost in a year, in the country as well as in the city! A person may lose the spirit of devotion to Christ; he may lose the sharp distinction of right from wrong; he may lose the readiness to give his service to needy causes. May we seek to recover any lost qualities of the Christian spirit.

O God, in the midst of busy lives, may the inward man be renewed. Amen.

Week 18—Day 7   **Read Luke 9:23-26**

Many people have said to outstanding Christians, "I would give anything to have your faith." They were wrong. They were not willing to give *anything.* For they might have had such a faith if they had been willing to pay the price. The only way to have the peace and power of Christian experience is to venture life on the truth of Christ. We cannot have peace and power merely by giving intellectual assent to statements of doctrine; we cannot have them by becoming learned in theology. We can have them only by venturing our life on the truth as it is in Christ, and by ordering our affairs on the principles which Jesus taught. That is not easy. In a world where men still worship mammon, it is hard to seek first the kingdom of God. The experiment will cost much, but in no other way can we have the experience which does bring peace and power, which Paul describes as "union with Christ."

O God, we seek a faith that will not shrink from paying the price of taking up our cross daily and following thee. Amen.

Out on a Limb

Week 19—Day 1   **Read Matt. 7:21-23**

In a small town in the United States last year grievous acts of racial injustice had been performed. Boys and girls were attacked by grown men. One of the prominent citizens of the town was shocked. He got to thinking about himself and what he had done to prevent such outrages. He sadly discovered that he had done very little. He said to a friend, "For twenty years I have sat here comfortably and never lifted a finger to help in such a situation. I am going out on a limb." He did exactly that. He made his witness clear, at considerable risk to his friendships and business. But he found that "going out on a limb" for a good cause is the most wonderful journey in the world.

We heed, O Lord, thy summons, and answer, "Here are we; send us upon thine errand; let us thy servants be." Amen.

Week 19—Day 2   **Read John 13:15-17**

There is a striking little poem entitled "The Out Trail." It tells of a woman employed at a travel agency who spent the day planning for people journeys to wonderful places but at five o'clock she shut up the office and timidly went to her home, from which she had never moved in all her life.

We may become like that, telling people about the wonderful places they can go in Christian effort, the adventures they may have in service, the joy that may be theirs in sacrifice, and yet never ourselves make such journeys.

Our Father God, may we always remember that our Savior said, "ye know these things. Happy are ye if ye do them." Lead us into the happiness of not only knowing thy will, but of doing it. Amen.

Week 19—Day 3   Read Gal. 6:9-10

A hazard we all meet again and again is the danger of getting discouraged. We often quit an effort because the chances of success seem small. It is a help to remember the people who by persistence have won out over discouragement. When Caruso's first singing teacher heard him, he said, "My friend, your voice sounds like the whistling of the wind through a window." But Caruso did not quit.

Help us to do thy works, O God, trusting the outcome to thee, and not giving up in the face of difficulties. Amen.

Week 19—Day 4   Read Luke 4:17-19

We read in Jesus' words at Nazareth that he was sent to "preach deliverance to the captives." Think today of the danger of unusual prisons from which people need to be delivered. Some people are prisoners of *time,* their interest is enclosed by the present hour and year. They are not concerned

95

with the high wisdom of yesterday or the possibilities of a better tomorrow. For them there is only one day—today.

Others are prisoners of *space*. They are bound to their own locality. They never lift their eyes for long from their own front yard. Jesus' words, "Go ye into all the world," mean nothing to them. They are chained.

Deliver us, O God, from any bondage that would prevent us from being fully committed servants of thine. For Jesus' sake.

Week 19—Day 5 Read Mark 1:14-25

Read as much of the first chapter of Mark as you can in the time you have. It is the amazing record of just a few days in the opening of Jesus' public ministry. Will you notice particularly the words "immediately" and "straightway." One meaning of "straightway" is "immediately." Notice that in fourteen verses this idea "immediately" occurs five times! This word, repeated so often, gives the sharp impression of urgency in the life and work of Jesus.

With this word "immediately," contrast words we so often use in connection with our duties, words such as "tomorrow," "after a while," "some day."

Help us, O God, to remember that thy business requires haste. May we give ourselves resolutely to the tasks that need to be done. Amen.

Dante, in his great poem, *The Divine Comedy,* has a wonderful pictorial passage which stresses the point that "neutrals" in the moral battle are worthless. Dante places the cowards and the irresolute folk in an "ante-hell" in a place which was peopled first by the angels who were neutral in the conflict between God and Satan. Are we neutral in the struggle to establish Christ's teaching in our society? Have we made a separate peace with forces of evil? God has no use for a neutral.

Keep us, O our Father, from trying to serve both God and Mammon. Help us to serve one master only, even Jesus Christ our Lord. Amen.

Willa Cather, the novelist, said that after writing the first draft of *O Pioneers!,* she ceased trying to *write* and gave herself completely to the business of *re-living* and recording the memory of people she had known.

Is not that our task in our religious life, to give ourselves completely to the business of re-living the memory of a person we have known, even Jesus Christ. If we do, people may take knowledge of us, that we resemble him.

Help us, O God, to keep bright and always visible the memory of all the best persons we have known. Amen.

The Most Dangerous Journey in the World

Week 20—Day 1   **Read Luke 18:1-8**

A lecturer was talking about what he called "the most dangerous journey in the world." Most people in the audience began to think of a journey into the African jungle, or facing shipwreck going through the Straits of Magellan. The lecturer explained: "More and more books are being sold about escaping from prison with a toothpick or journeying up the Amazon on stilts. But the most dangerous journey is the journey of our day-to-day living. It is dangerous because it always ends in death!"

Our day-to-day living is dangerous for other reasons. We face temptations. We are liable to become discouraged and lose heart. We meet troubles. For this dangerous journey we need the renewing of our minds by communion with God.

May we begin and end each day in fellowship with thee, O God. Amen.

Week 20—Day 2   **Read I Pet. 5:6-9**

The more the outward world is threatening and terrifying, the more we stand in need of those internal resources which alone can buttress our personal lives against the pressure of discouragement and fear. Our bodies can stand the pressure of fifteen pounds on every square inch, only because there is an inward pressure also. So we need the internal resources of faith which will be able to withstand the pressure which events exert on our spirits. That is the meaning of the great exhortation of Paul in Ephesians, "Taking the shield of faith wherewith ye shall be able to quench all the fiery darts of the wicked."

Strengthen our hearts to face with courage all that may befall us along an unknown trail. Lead us in faith and hope and love. Amen.

Week 20—Day 3   **Read Matt. 5:17-19**

A little girl had reached the high point in school when she was being initiated into the wonders of arithmetic. Minus signs, plus signs, and division signs had made a deep impression on her. One day in church she looked intently at a gold cross on the altar. She whispered to her father, "What is the plus sign doing on the altar?" In one way she had her sign confused, but in a far deeper sense she was absolutely right! *The cross is a plus sign.* The redemption pictured by the cross has put a big plus sign into life. It has made "plus" men and women, that is, people *plus* the power of God's love revealed on the cross.

O God Eternal, who dost desire us to grow into likeness to thee, steady our unsteadfastness and guide us day by day in thy ways. Amen.

There are two kinds of strength, both needed in the Christian life—strength to *do* and strength to *endure*. Often it is harder to endure, just to "stand" for things that are difficult or painful, than it is to act. Consider the lightship, anchored to one spot to keep a light burning to guide ships away from danger. The crew has to stand and take any kind of weather that comes. It is much more desirable to be on a great liner which plows through the seas than on a lightship which does not "plow" anywhere. Both kinds of strength are needed in God's work. In our scripture reference we read of the power to endure, to "stand" things which they could not change, shown by so many of the Christian martyrs. "They also serve who only stand and wait."

O God, our Father, direct our hearts into the patience of Christ. Strengthen us by thy grace to endure trials. Amen.

When we get to feeling that all trouble which we have is a total calamity, it is well to read the fourth psalm. Consider this statement in prayer: "Thou hast enlarged me when I was in distress." Think of being enlarged when in distress. Our first thought may well be, "Fantastic!" But that is what so often happened. Out of deep distress, men and women have been enlarged in mind and spirit. Out of their very sorrow they have been able to render large service to others in need. Call to mind how the soul of Helen Keller was enlarged by her blindness. Sorrow has enabled many people to bring comfort and strength to others.

Grant that we, O God, passing the valley of sorrow may make it a place of strength. Amen.

Week 20—Day 6   **Read Ps. 86:11-13, 15-17**

We are often tempted to feel that the best achievements of people have happened when conditions were favorable. We feel that they have happened when the person can sing, "Oh, what a beautiful morning! Everything's going my way." History shows us that that is not true. Some of the very greatest gifts to the race have come from days of trials and tribulations. Here is one of the most familiar examples. When we listen to the "Hallelujah Chorus," we think Handel must have written it on a day when everything was going well. But he wrote it when his health and fortunes had failed, when his creditors were threatening him with imprisonment, and he was at the very lowest point in his life. We have our "low" days. Life is not on a level. It goes up and down. But remember that in the midst of difficulties God brings great achievement.

May we be heartened onward, O God, by the remembrance that thou dost move in a mysterious way thy wonders to perform. May we trust thee. Amen.

Week 20—Day 7   **Read John 8:30-32**

It is reported that the most familiar question on Broadway where playwrights often meet is, "How's your

101

second act?" In writing a play the second act is the hardest.
The first act is fairly easy. The writer introduces the characters,
the setting is impressed on the audience, the main plot is begun.
But the second act means going on with the plot. That is hard.
Isn't the same true in life? It is easy to make a start on some
good undertaking. It is hard to keep going on; hard to develop
beyond the beginnings. For that we need the "grace of continuance."

*Grant, O God, that we may not turn back after putting our
hands to the plow, but may continue in thy service. Amen.*

Great Invitations

Week 21—Day 1   **Read Matt. 22:1-9**

        Consider today the people who made light
of the king's invitation to a wedding feast. It was a very high
honor, but the guests who were bidden "made light of it!"
(Matt. 22:5)

What a blunder they made! But let us think of great "invitations" which we may make light of if we are thoughtless.
There are the great invitations to see the beauties and wonders
of nature. There are the great invitations to all of us to share
the thoughts of great souls in reading. Above these, there are
God's invitations to hold communion with him and to become
workers with him in the blessing of lives. Do we make light of
these?

*Give us alert ears and minds, that when we hear thy voice
we may readily respond. Amen.*

Week 21—Day 2   **Read Matt. 7:21**

        The question is often asked, "Why did the
League of Nations fail when it was created with such high
hopes after World War I? A strong League of Nations might
have prevented the Second World War." James Hilton, in his
novel *Random Harvest* gives a reasonable and arresting ex-

planation. He diagnosed the trouble in one shining phrase, "There was public approval without private faith." Too many nations and individuals gave "public approval" but gave no real private faith.

Religion is also weak in the lives of individuals, from the same cause, "public approval without private faith." Is that true of us? Public approval is easy; private faith is difficult.

O for a faith that will not shrink though pressed by every foe, that will not tremble on the brink of any earthly woe. Amen.

Week 21—Day 3   **Read Heb. 12:14-16**

A recent cartoon presents a question which all of us might very well face. A man is pictured looking out of a library window. All four walls are lined with books. Books and magazines cover the tables. It is a rainy day and the man looks out at the rain and says, "What on earth can a man do on a day like this?"

The question is so absurd it is funny! Couldn't the poor simpleton think of reading as something to do? Yet we are liable to ask, "What can I do in a place like this?" and we may overlook the opportunities for the growth of our own souls which our location offers us, and the opportunities for helpful service to many people. We may be as stupid as the man in the library!

Help us, our Father, to see that there are lonely hearts to cherish and people to help as the days are going by. Amen.

Consider this observation by Sydney Smith, "You will find people ready enough to act the good Samaritan without the oil and twopence." There is little need to comment on that! It strikes home. The good Samaritan was willing to see his helpfulness clear through to the finish, even when it cost him something.

Help us, O God, to give our thought and strength to the needs of others, not grudgingly or of necessity, but swiftly and gladly. Amen.

Think of the parable of the rich man and the beggar Lazarus. The rich man is usually called Dives. We usually think of the sin of Dives as selfish hard-heartedness. It may not have been that directly. The real sin of Dives was that he was blind to what was before his eyes. There was the beggar on his doorstep. Dives passed by him every day and never saw him! We may say, "Impossible!" but it is possible. We are all in danger of doing exactly that. We do not need to be rich to commit that sin. Every one of us may fail to see what is right before our eyes. There may be people in need, people who are lonely, the sick who need help, the tempted who need support. Do we pass by every day, absorbed in ourselves, and do nothing?

Open our eyes, O God, that we may be quick to see the need right in front of us, and quick to respond. Amen.

Rebecca West, the novelist, has written that "it is the greatest sin to deal with people as if they were *things.*" That depersonalizes people. It takes away their birthright as human beings and as children of God. That was the essential sin of slavery. It made convenient and profitable *things* out of people. That is the sin of an employer who regards workers as "hands." That is *our* sin, whenever we try to use people just as *things* for our advantage.

Save us, O God, from the sin of looking at people as merely means to an end we have chosen, and not as persons with a priceless value to thee. Amen.

A fairly rich man was boasting not long ago to a group of friends that he watched very carefully not to waste money by giving to what might be unworthy people. "Yes sir," he said complacently, "I have never been taken in." A friend said to him kindly, "Perhaps that is what is the matter with you. Perhaps because you never take a risk in helping a case of need, you have never been really 'taken in' to the human family as a genuine member; perhaps you have never been 'taken in' to any loving heart, but have remained outside." How about it?

Make our ears quick to hear the still sad music of humanity, and our hearts quick to respond. Amen.

WEEK 22

Distant Early Warning

Week 22—Day 1   **Read Prov. 22:3**

Have you ever heard of the "D.E.W." line?
It has nothing to do with moisture that settles on the ground
in the early morning. The initials "D.E.W." stand for Distant
Early Warning. They are the farthest north of three radar
fences which span great cities in the United States and the
North Pole, to give warning of approaching planes.

There ought to be some things parallel to that for warning
of approaching evil in personal life. There *is* such a warning
system. Jesus taught us to pray, "Deliver us from evil." We can
be warned by testing every possible action by the spirit of
Christ.

*Help us to watch and pray that we enter not into temptation.
For Jesus' sake. Amen.*

Week 22—Day 2   **Read Matt. 13:5-6, 20-21**

Jesus in his parable of the sower lays great
stress on roots. He said of the seed that fell in stony places,
"Because they had no root they withered away." He said that
the person who had no root in himself endures only a short
time.

It is very disturbing that ours has been called a "rootless

107

generation." A large number of Americans are wanderers on the face of the country. More than that, many people are rootless in that they do not sink down roots into a body of belief and conviction. They have no high tradition which sustains them. We all face the danger of "having no root." The way of life is to be "rooted and grounded in him."

May we draw out strength for living from deep sources. O God. May we be rooted in a rich faith. Amen.

Week 22—Day 3   **Read Eph. 5:15**

We hear the advice given endlessly usually as an excuse for moral laxity of conduct, "When in Rome, do as the Romans do." But often we do not ask, as we should, "Which Romans? the poor, the middle class, the rich? the clergy? the men who sell bananas? the Communists? the Pope?" They are all in Rome. We have to choose for ourselves. We are not compelled to follow a multitude to do evil. We can choose the best in any company. We can say in any situation, "As for me and my house, we will serve the Lord."

Grant, O God, that we may have the strength of character to resist all pressures to lower our moral standards of action. Amen.

Week 22—Day 4   **Read I Tim. 6:12, 20**

Winston Churchill at a service of baptism of his grandchild "sat with tears streaming down his cheeks. 'Poor infant,' he murmured, 'to be born in such a world as this!'" We can all understand that depressed feeling. But may we bear in mind two considerations arising from the fact that ours is a dangerous world. First, it is God's world. He has not left it. Our trust is in his love and power. Second, we are called to be workers with God for making a better world.

Grant unto us, O God, reliance upon thee and direction from thee for all our efforts. Amen.

Week 22—Day 5   **Read Rom. 15:1-6**

A recent article in a magazine entitled "Throw-Away Living" describes the extent to which we are living in an age of "disposables." Not only tin cans but almost all kinds of utensils are made to be thrown away: napkins, tablecloths, paper dishes, "away with them" when we get through! One man has suggested solving the parking problem in cities by "disposable cars" which can be thrown away when the city is reached! But there is a different and more serious kind of "throw-away living" in which many people are indulging today. People are throwing away the moral and religious convictions and principles which are needed for the finest kind of living. We cannot throw away the teaching of Jesus and make a successful navigation of life's seas.

Give us strength, O God, and the determination to hold fast to that which is good, that we may not receive the gift of the grace of God in vain. Amen.

One of the great absorbing interests today, especially of children, is the conquest of space. Boys and girls with "space cadet" suits are ready to take off for the moon any day. One volume of science fiction stories is entitled *New Tales of Space and Time*.

But far more important for every person and for the whole world of humanity are the *old* tales of space and time. Here is the old tale of space, always new: that there is no place distant from the love of God. That is declared in the 139th Psalm: "If I take the wings of the morning, and dwell in the uttermost parts of the sea, even there shall thy hand lead me, and thy right hand shall hold me." That is something to hold to anywhere.

Strengthen our faith, O God, to know that no place is a Godforsaken place, that thou art everywhere. Amen.

To every one of the temptations of Jesus, He said an emphatic, "Get out!" He could do that because he could hear another voice saying. "You must!" The tempter tried to break down his realization about who he was. Satan said, *"If* thou be the son of God." Jesus knew he was God's son, and so he could say, "Get thee hence." If we keep strong in our minds the words of our Father, "You must!" we can say to evil suggestions, "Get out!"

May nothing break down in us, O God, the remembrance that thou art our Father and that we must do what is pleasing to thee. Amen.

110

What God Hath Joined Together

Week 23—Day 1   **Read John 9:1-4**

We all know that in the marriage service there are the words, "What God hath joined together, let man not put asunder!" That applies to other things than marriage. There has been too great a separation between work and religion, for instance. Work and religion belong together. The noted historian, Arnold Toynbee, has within recent days made a strong plea to bring religion back into closer relation to our daily work. He said, "The problem as I see it, is to keep our work, when once we have consecrated it, in that subordinate relation to our religion to which the very act of consecration has dedicated it."

Help us, O God, to bring to our work the remembrance that the night is coming when man's work is done. Amen.

Week 23—Day 2   **Read Matt. 25:31-34**

We are accustomed to the expression, "sheep and goats," as representing good and bad people, the sheep representing the good and the goats representing the bad. Thus, in the last judgment, the king puts the sheep who are all rewarded for good action, on one side, and the goats, who are all punished for bad action, on the other side.

111

A visitor to Palestine noticed one difference between sheep and goats. The sheep will follow a leader but the goats have to be driven. Think that over! Will we follow leadership in a good cause, or do we have to be driven?

Help us, O God, to respond to the call of our Master, "Follow me." Amen.

Week 23—Day 3   Read Mark 12:28-30

We all know the statement, "My mind to me a kingdom is." That is what a mind ought to be, a kingdom with a ruler in control. Without a dominant purpose a mind can become a chaos, where one desire pushes another, and there is no discipline. The mind becomes an uncontrolled riot.

We are told to "love God with the mind." When we do that, when we bring all the powers of our minds to the love and obedience of God, our mind does become a kingdom, where life is not dissipated but brought under one purpose and rule.

Help us, O God, to put our wayward thoughts and desires under the control of thy will and purpose. Amen.

Week 23—Day 4   Read II Cor. 13:4-5

A British author, speaking of the Christian religion, once said that he thought he could have been a great believer. A friend who knew him well commented on that, in a not unkindly spirit, that he did not think his friend "had quite courage enough to be a great believer."

A great believer is not one who can rattle off the creeds of the church from memory and say to all of them, "I believe." A great believer is one who cares greatly about his belief and makes his relation to God the first thing in his life. A great believer is one who has courage to act on his belief.

We thank thee, O God, for thy great revelation of thyself and thy will for us. Grant that our faith may not be in words only but in deed. In the name of our Lord and Saviour. Amen.

Week 23—Day 5   **Read Matt. 6:19-21**

The newspapers have been full of advertisements of so-called "self-help books." One recent one proclaimed itself a sure-fire help to "get what you want." The simple-minded buyer would conclude that with this book as his guide, the world would be his. The advertisement promises "how to think big and be big," and "how to forge ahead." Those two words tell the story—"ahead" and "big." So many people want to be "big shots" and get ahead of other people. The whole emphasis is wrong. What we need to seek is not "how to get what I want" but to seek to know and realize *what God wants* us to be, and to do.

Grant, O God, that in all our days, we may seek first thy kingdom and righteousness. In Jesus' name. Amen.

Week 23—Day 6   **Read Phil. 3:10**

There is a tendency in our days to reverse the prayer of the Pharisee in Jesus' parable of the Pharisee and the publican. The Pharisee thanked the Lord that he was "not as other men." We tend, as someone has said, to thank the Lord that we *are* as other men. In these days when so many forces are at work to compel conformity to the ways of the majority, we are tempted to try to be "regular fellows," just like everyone else.

That is not the kind of follower Jesus wants. He asks for undivided allegiance to him, no matter how different from the ways of the world.

May we give constant ear to thy call, O God, which bids us to seek first the kingdom of God. Amen.

Week 23—Day 7   Read Isa. 40:29-31

This meditation is particularly addressed to all the "old folks"—over twenty-one!

There is a fine ideal to strive for in the description given by Theodore Roosevelt of Senator Thomas H. Benton of Missouri. He said Mr. Benton at the age of seventy-six had "reached a level of moral grandeur that he had never touched before, and few indeed are the politicians who reach old age and disappear from view still rising." A great picture—to reach old age and "disappear from view still rising." Never quit! Keep on rising!

Grant, O God, that with thy continuing grace, we may go from strength to strength, better servants of thine year by year. In Jesus' name. Amen.

Enough for Incidentals

Week 24—Day 1   **Read Ps. 124:1-8**

A young wife made a comment on budget books with which young couples often struggle, which will strike a responsive chord in the minds of many people. She said, "None of the budget books ever allow enough for incidentals." Haven't we all learned the truth of that? It is the unexpected expenses, arriving suddenly and without being prepared for, which knock out the budget.

We must work to make allowances for "incidentals" in our spiritual life. We must be prepared for unscheduled demands on our spiritual strength and resources. The swift temptation which meets us unawares, the heavy load that must be endured—these demand a life reinforced by prayer and communion with God.

Our Father, may we daily seek thy gifts of strength that through all the strains and stresses we may be more than conquerors. Amen.

Week 24—Day 2   **Read Matt. 6:9-13**

Two centuries ago and even later, the belief in witches was quite common. One of the superstitions about witches was that they recited the Lord's Prayer backwards.

That was supposed to be a blasphemous thing to do and brought a punishment with it. No one I know of recites the Lord's Prayer backwards. But many people do turn the prayer around and use it backward in their practical life. That is, they put their own needs first, their desires come before the worship of God. Many people think first, "Give us this day our daily bread," before they say, "Our Father, hallowed be Thy name." In that way we can put ourselves before God. In the prayer given by Jesus, God comes first.

Our Father who art in heaven, hallowed be they name. Thy kingdom come, thy will be done in my life as it is in heaven. Amen.

Week 24—Day 3   **Read Matt. 6:9-13**

The Reverend Lyman Abbott once gave a vivid demonstration of what faith in God means in life. He wrote a version of the Lord's Prayer with all reference to God left out. This is what he wrote: "Our Brethren who are on the earth, Hallowed be our name. Our Kingdom come, Our will be done, for there is no heaven. We must get this day our daily bread; We neither forgive nor are forgiven. We fear not temptation, for we deliver ourselves from evil. For ours is the kingdom and the power, for there is no glory and no forever." Measure the distance from that to the Lord's "Our Father Who Art in Heaven." The prayer without God is a cold, bleak prayer; the world without God is a cold, bleak world.

Grant, our Father, that we may never allow prayer to become a formal, lifeless thing—but that it may be the meeting of spirit with Spirit. Amen.

116

One problem comes to all of us, or at least to most of us—how to deal with low spirits. Unless we have some spiritual resources to bring to bear on our spirits, we are liable to be sunk in gloom. Thomas Gray, the poet, wrote in a letter: "Low spirits are my true and faithful companions. They get up with me and go to bed with me, make journeys and returns as I do." George Eliot, the novelist, once said: "My address is Grief Castle, on the River of Gloom, in the Valley of Sadness." But low spirits can be lifted by a confident trust in God. By the practice of prayer low spirits can be transformed.

May we remember, O God, to cast all our care upon thee. Amen.

Many thoughtful students of the Bible have pointed out the great difference between two kinds of prayer. One begins with the words, "Give me." The other begins, "Give us." There are times, of course, when we must pray in the singular number. We must say, "God be merciful to *me,* a sinner." We must say, "Receive *my* thanks," and "Help *me* to be true." But prayer should be for the large part in the plural number. Prayer at its best says, in the words of the Lord's prayer, "Give *us* this day our daily bread." It says, "Forgive *us* our debts." It says, "Deliver *us* from evil." After this manner pray ye in the plural, for the whole family of God.

We pray not for ourselves alone, O God, but for all thy children. Amen.

In the English publication *Who's Who* each person whose biography is included in the volume is asked to put down his favorite hobby. A writer, William Sansom, gave his hobby as "watching." It is a good hobby, a good recreation. A large part of the history of science has been achieved by watching. Copernicus watched the sky and became convinced that the earth moved. Harvey watched the veins and arteries in the body and discovered the circulation of the blood.

Think what devoted watching will do in our religious life. Jesus said, "Watch and pray." Watch for the beauty of God's world. Watch for opportunities to help people in need. Watch our step that we do not fall into temptation.

May we watch and pray that we do not forget thee, O God. Amen.

Do you ever make engagements with yourself? You make them with nearly everyone else, the butcher, the baker, the candlestick maker (or electric light company). Why not make an engagement with yourself? Surely in our time "The world is too much with us, late and soon." We lose all our powers while we get and spend. In many ways our generation has declared war on solitude and meditation and reading. Today it is hard to make a place and time to be alone. So many of our gadgets, such as portable TV and radio, are designed to prevent us from ever being alone. Everyday make a regular place and time to come face to face with God and yourself for such solitude prepares us to bring something of great value to the world.

Take thou our minds, dear Lord, we humbly pray. Give us the mind of Christ each passing day. Amen.

A Pillar of Fire

Week 25—Day 1   **Read Exod. 13:20-22**

John Jay Chapman, an American writer, has written this about the Bible, "The Bible is a luminous congregation of vapors, a cloud by day and a pillar of fire by night, and the darker the skies grow, whether above an epoch or an individual, the more light it emits." That is a good sentence to remember, in these days when the skies "above our epoch" have dark clouds. But God's truth shines in dark epochs, and it is the duty of all Christians to do all in their power to bring the light of the Bible into our days. To do that well, we must first let that light shine in our hearts.

A glory gilds the sacred page, O God. Help us to see that glory on the pages of Scripture, and to let it shine in our lives and into the world. Amen.

Week 25—Day 2   **Read Mark 6:30, 31, 45**

A book designed to help the reader to acquire a larger stock of words was published a few years ago. At the top of the advertisement for the book was this sentence, "Anyone can have a great vocabulary." Doubtless that is true. New words can be added to one's store by study and memory.

Think over that sentence, however, in relation to the language in which religious faith talks. That is what the Bible is really all about. It puts great words on our lips because the gospel puts great realities in our life. Here are some words of a truly great vocabulary: "The Lord is my shepherd," "Now are we the sons of God." Make these words your own!

Help us, O God, to keep thy Word fresh and available in our minds, that it may give light and leading to us at all times. Amen.

Week 25—Day 3   **Read Lev. 25:10**

Here is one of the truest, finest things ever said about the Bible. Young Martin Luther's teacher told him: "Leave the Bible alone. It creates unrest."

The man who said that was warning against reading the Bible. Actually, he was giving, although he did not know it, one of the strong reasons for reading the Bible. It does create "unrest," thank God! The high moral and spiritual teachings of the Bible create unrest in us, in that we become dissatisfied with ourselves. That moves us to strive to become better. The teachings of the Bible create unrest against tyranny and the denial of liberty—a blessed unrest.

We thank thee, our Father, for every word that quickens our desire to become better and stronger persons. Amen.

Week 25—Day 4   **Read Ps. 46:1-5**

A few years ago, in a book in the Rivers of America series entitled *The Monongahela*, Richard Bissell wrote: "In order to have a river in your blood, you have to work on her for wages. You don't get to know a river by riding along its banks in a car taking snapshots, or by going down it in a canoe with a patent cookstove, or by reading books about it. . . . You've got to eat it, sleep it, and breathe it, until you've got river in your shoe soles."

Hold those true words in mind, in connection with the beautiful phrase in Ps. 46, "There is a river, the streams whereof shall make glad the city of God." We do not know the river of refreshment and strengthening, which flows in the Bible, by turning a few pages once in a while. We must live with it.

Grant, O God, that the entrance of thy word may give light to our minds. Amen.

Week 25—Day 5   Read Ps. 119:89-93

An English journalist has told of his running away from home at the age of fifteen. He said that he spent part of his precious store of money for two books of poetry. "For," he said, "I knew I would need good reading for a dismal journey."

No doubt, running away from home would be a "dismal journey." There come times when life, for a time at least, seems dismal. The road leads up hill; we lose friends; our purposes are broken off. The Bible has been very good reading for "a dismal journey." It will be a light on our path in darkness, and a rod and a staff to comfort us. But, yet, if it is to be a constant help, it must go with us. Just to keep it handy, or to reach it every six months, won't help much!

Whether we walk by green pastures and still waters, or in dangerous, dismal places, O God, may we be sustained by thy word and thy companionship. In the name of our Lord. Amen.

Week 25—Day 6   Read Prov. 13:34

Here is a novelist and journalist saying a tremendously important thing about the danger to our country and the world of blurring the difference between right and wrong. Sterling North writes in the *New York World—Telegram:*

"Personally I do not see how civilization can survive if we continue to blur the difference between right and wrong; if we scorn all the ethical lessons learned so painfully by the human race; if we insist upon the values of Babylon slyly promoted as the values of Christianity.

"To remind us that we should lift our eyes to the hills I suggest a rereading of the Book we buy most frequently but never find the time to read."

We bring our thanks, O God, for the clear powerful teaching in the Bible on the difference between right and wrong. May we make time to keep that difference uppermost in our minds. Amen.

Week 25—Day 7   Read Isa. 62:10

A well-known newspaper correspondent, Quentin Reynolds, said this about the Bible: "If I were a dictator the first book I would burn would be the Bible, I'd burn it because I'd realize that the whole concept of democracy came from that book. 'Democracy' is a Greek word which means rule by the people, but even at the height of its ancient glory Athens was not a democracy. The Greeks gave us a word for it, but the Bible gave us the philosophy for the way of life."

Help us, O God, to give mind and heart and strength to the preservation of the truths of the Bible as the ruling power in our nation's life. In Jesus' name. Amen.

WEEK 26

The Power of Continuance

Week 26—Day 1   Read Rev. 3:12

There is a story of a young boxer in Australia which both brings a smile and also makes a strong point. He was in a prize fight with a strong opponent. After the fight he telegraphed his father, "Won easily in eighty-four rounds."

The smile comes from the realization that it took him eighty-four rounds to win the fight "easily"! But we admire the persistence to keep going for a long, long time until he won.

That shows the value of "hanging on." Too many efforts for good are given up too soon. Victories in the fight for righteousness depend on the power of continuance.

Grant that all our works may be begun and continued in thee. In the name and spirit of Jesus. Amen.

Week 26—Day 2   Read Isa. 61:1-3

An art lover has written that very often a dim sky makes a better background for rich colors than a bright blue sky. He writes, "A bright blue sky is of necessity the highlight of the picture, and its brightness kills all the bright blue flowers. But on a gray day, the larkspur looks like fallen Heaven, the red daisies are really the last red eyes of the day." Think how many beautiful qualities of life have been found under a "dim sky." Sorrow has come into life, but it has not

125

ruined life. Courage, patience, sympathy, and many truly Christlike qualities have been developed in sorrow and grief and difficulty.

When sorrow and grief meet us, O God, grant that we may not be overwhelmed or made bitter, but may we accept them in trust to thee. In Jesus' name. Amen.

Week 26—Day 3   Read Isa. 40:29-31

An advertisement of an auto repair garage appears quite regularly in the newspaper of an eastern city. The advertisement proclaims in large letters, "Defective Clutches Repaired." That could be very important. When a car is rolling along swiftly, it is important to have dependable clutches!

Firm "clutches" are essential in any kind of journey. We need to have a grip on ourselves and our appetites strong enough to hold them in check and keep them from running our lives into the ditch. For that we need the help of him of whom it is written, "He giveth power to the faint."

Help us, O God, to keep our desires disciplined, that we may bring all our powers to thy service. Amen.

Week 26—Day 4   Read Matt. 26:26-30

"When they had sung an hymn, they went out." That is a vivid picture of spiritual fortification of mind and heart for great endurance. That happened to Jesus. It can, by the grace of God, happen to us. We can be sure that, as the disciples and Jesus left the room where the Last Supper was held, they did not sing a song of jollification. They did not sing the first century equivalent of "Hail, Hail, the Gang's All Here." We can be pretty sure what they sang. It very probably was the Passover Hymn, the second part of the Hillel, which was always sung at the conclusion of the Passover service, Ps. 115-18. These psalms have a great triumphal note, "O trust in the Lord." Put a great word of trust in your heart in the morning. Then you can go out empowered for any unknown or known demand.

Help us each day, God, to remember the words of Christ, "Lo, I am with you alway." Strengthen us with renewed commitments to thee. Amen.

Week 26—Day 5   **Read Job 4:4; Eph. 3:14**

Have you ever thought how many references to knees there are in the Bible? Fear is reflected in knees which give way. Thus in Job 4:4, thanks are given to God: "Thou hast strengthened the feeble knees." Life is hard on the knees. It brings to all of us in some degree tasks and struggles which are hard to stand up to. Our knees are liable to buckle under us in fear or weakness. There is one sure cure for "feeble knees." It is, appropriately enough, in the knees! Courage, stamina, and endurance against shock come from prayer, from bending the knees in prayer to God. Paul pictures this—"for this cause I bow my knees."

Companion us, O God, this day, throughout our various tasks

*and pleasures, and garrison our feet with light, and our hearts
with love. Amen.*

Week 26—Day 6   **Read Rom. 12:1-3**

Margaret Mead, the anthropologist, who has
studied the lives of people in all parts of the world, made an
acute observation on life and manners in the United States.
She spoke sadly of what she called "the flattening out of our
language and culture to find a common denominator." It is
happening in many places. People get afraid of saying or doing
anything which is not being said or done by the majority of
their circle. They use language which marks them as "regular
fellows"; they try to find a common denominator of conduct. So
they attempt nothing that is not being done by the common
herd. Is this happening to us?

*Help us, O God, to keep in our common speech and life, the
words and acts of our great heritage of faith in the Lord Jesus
Christ. Amen.*

Week 26—Day 7   **Read Phil. 4:10-14**

Here is a passage from a beautiful little book
by Langston Hughes, on life in Harlem, titled, strangely
enough, *The Sweet Sticky Flypaper of Life:* "When the bicycle of the Lord bearing His Messenger with a telegram for
Sister Mary Bradley, saying 'Come Home,' arrived at 113 West
134th Street, New York City, Sister Bradley said, 'Boy, take

that wire right back to St. Peter, because I'm not prepared to go. I might be a little sick, but I ain't no wise tired.'"

It's a great way to live, to be in "no wise tired." Read what Paul has reported: "I have learned to be content," and "cast down but not destroyed." Paul had a rough life, imprisonment, riots, stoning. Yet he was "in no wise tired" of life. Here is an old way to keep from being tired: "They that wait upon the Lord shall renew their strength; they shall mount up with wings as eagles; they shall run, and not be weary; they shall walk, and not faint" (Isa. 40:31). Millions have tried that successfully.

Grant that we may have such a genuine faith in thee, O God, that we may be strong for all things. Amen.

WEEK 27

A Green Thumb

Week 27—Day 1   **Read Luke 19:1-8**

Among gardeners a very common expression is, "He has a green thumb." Some people seem gifted with an uncanny ability to make things grow. Some devoted people can toil terribly over a plot of ground and seem to raise nothing but witch grass and weeds. Others stroke the ground, touch it here and there, and it becomes a sort of Garden of Eden! This is a gift. But there is a richer gift, a "green thumb" for people! That achievement is to have personal relationships with people that help their best qualities grow. While some people touch the lives of other people with what seem to be gloved and clammy hands, other folks by their contact make them more alive. Think over how Jesus brought out the best in the people he met. Zacchaeus is a fine example of that.

O lead me, Lord, that I may lead the wandering and the wavering feet. O feed me, Lord, that I may feed the hungering ones with manna sweet. Amen.

Week 27—Day 2   **Read Ps. 57:7-11**

Those are great words in our selection for today, "My heart is fixed." But note that they do not mean, "My brain has become hard as a rock." A fixed heart is one that trusts supremely in God. But a petrified brain is one so solid that a new idea cannot enter it. The Pharisees in Jesus' time were very violently opposed to his healing on the Sabbath. It was not, as they thought, a case of their heart being "fixed." It was the "fixed" mind, so hard they could not see a work of mercy was a blessed thing, in any day. We should say, "My heart is fixed" in trust in God. But also remember that Jesus said, "Thou shalt love God with thy *mind*."

May we love thee, O God, with all our soul and strength and mind, and dedicate all our powers to thy service. Amen.

Week 27—Day 3   **Read Mark 12:38-40**

"What things make you maddest?" Think it over for a few minutes. One man has said recently that this question is a test of our character. Do we get "maddest" at some slight to ourselves, our failure to get prestige or as much profit as others? Do we turn angry at being a "big shot" or at what we call "getting behind in the procession"? Or do we get mad at injustice inflicted on other people, oppression and the causing of suffering?

Grant, O God, that we may share right now the concern of Christ for others. Amen.

Week 27—Day 4   **Read Luke 8:24-25**

Jesus is reported in the Gospels as saying to his disciples. "Oh, ye of little faith." They had faith enough to leave their occupations and homes and follow him, didn't they?

131

Wasn't that enough? Evidently not. Jesus asked for undivided allegiance. Half-and-half discipleship was not enough. Could Jesus call us "ye of little faith"? Consider these dangers mentioned in the *Evanston Report* of the World Council of Churches: "The dangers are complacency, lack of imagination and the dull sense of hopelessness that settles upon those of little faith."

Has this happened to us?

We thank thee, O God, that thou hast called us out of our darkness into thy marvelous light. Increase our faith in thee. Amen.

Week 27—Day 5   **Read Matt. 12:48-49**

Let us meditate today on the danger of living in too small a world. Consider the passage of Matthew's gospel which tells of Jesus' mother and brothers coming to see him. The disciples told Jesus that his mother and brothers wished to see him. He replied that the people around him were his mother and brothers.

That seems a harsh answer. It was not. It was Jesus' way of saying that beyond his own immediate family, there was the larger family of God, whom he must serve as well as his own family. For each of us, beyond the loving haven of home, there is a world of need we must live in and serve.

Save us, O God, from the confining walls of selfishness. May we always hear the word of Christ, "Go ye into all the world." Amen.

Here is a sentence worth remembering, particularly when tempted to be angry! "It is much easier to give a person a piece of your mind than it is to give the whole of your heart." Remember that when you start to give a person "a piece of your mind." Give the whole of your heart, for Jesus said, "Love your enemies." Also, a soft answer turneth away wrath.

May we set a guard upon our tongue and keep our words filled with the spirit of Christ. In his name, we pray. Amen.

Think about the good to others which comes from the right timing. A word of comfort for instance, counts for more when it is given at the time of greatest need. Help when the hour of need is at hand is far, far more help than that which straggles in when the need is past. The Good Samaritan did not say to the wounded man, "I'll stop on my next trip." He stopped to help then and there.

Can you think of any act of kindness to someone, about which you have thought, "I must do that sometime"? Remember the power of timing. "In season, how good it is!"

Save us, O God, from the failing of putting good works off, so that many of them never get done. Amen.

The Fifth Gospel

Week 28—Day 1   **Read II Cor. 3:2**

A newspaper cable from London, Oct. 8, 1956, contained this item of news: "London.—British newspapers report today that seven world experts on early Christianity and forgotten languages are working in a Cairo museum on ancient manuscripts—possibly on the fifth gospel—containing new sayings of Jesus Christ." Looking for a fifth written gospel at this late date is like looking for the pot of gold at the foot of the rainbow! But there is a *real* fifth gospel, a powerful gospel in persuasion. It has been known since the earliest days of Christianity. It is the gospel in our lives, the gospel proclaimed by our words and acts. Many people never read the Gospels in the Bible, but they do see the gospel proclaimed by those who can say, "It is no longer I that live, but Christ liveth in me."

Our Father, may we so demonstrate the power of Christ in our lives that others who see and hear us may take knowledge of us that we have been with Jesus. Amen.

Week 28—Day 2   **Read II Cor. 3:2-5**

A woman, after reading a book of Sherlock Holmes stories, said that she did not know how much she ought to thank the illustrator, as well as the author, for the vividness of the personality of the detective, Sherlock Holmes. Often in a book we owe much to the man who drew the pictures. Think how this is true of the Tenniel pictures of *Alice in Wonderland.*

It is true in the Christian religion, also. We are all immeasurably in debt to the great Author, the God who revealed himself in Christ. But hosts of men and women are deeply indebted to the "illustrator," the persons who in their own selves and actions have illustrated clearly the spirit of Christ, so that it becomes vivid in their own lives. As Paul said, "We are epistles, known and read of men." What kind of illustrations do we give of the gospels?

Grant, O God, that those who know us and the life we live, may find in our spirit and actions illustrations of the love of God. Amen.

Week 28—Day 3   Read Acts 7:54-59

          In the novel dealing with early Christianity, *The Robe* by Lloyd Douglas, there is a dramatic scene in which Demetrius, a Roman soldier, watches the stoning of Stephen. Just before his death, when Stephen looked up into Heaven and called upon God, the soldier was deeply moved, and said with conviction, "That man is looking at something!" The strongest persuasion we can give for our faith is to create the conviction in those who see our lives, that we are looking at something real! We convince others by the sincerity and power of our lives that we endure as seeing him who is invisible.

135

Help us, O God, to live so that others may be convinced that our faith is a sustaining power. Amen.

Week 28—Day 4   Read John 1:35-42

Consider the picture of far-reaching power in this thirty-seventh verse—the power of an overheard conversation. John the Baptist exclaimed about Jesus, "Behold the lamb of God!" Then we read, "And the two disciples heard him speak, and they followed Jesus." John was not talking to the two disciples. They just overheard him. What impression would people get from overhearing much of our conversation? Could there be anything finer in life than that people who overheard our daily conversation might "follow Jesus"?

O God, we dedicate our lips and tongues to thee. Grant that what people hear from us, when we are not consciously on display, may lead them to follow Jesus. Amen.

Week 28—Day 5   Read Isa. 40:9

We are all interested in cities, for cities influence the character and destiny of our nation. Consider this cry of Isaiah to his country: "Say to the cities of Judah, behold your God." That expresses the deepest need of cities in our time and nation. That is not what many cities are asking for as their greatest need. Bishop Gerald Kennedy says that there are only two questions asked in an American city. One is, "How can I reduce?" and the other is, "Where can I park?" Cities are clamoring for many things, other than to behold God. But that

136

is the need that underlies all others. Our task is to say to cities, "Behold your God," so that in obedience to God who has revealed himself in the life and teaching of Jesus Christ, cities may find the things that belong to their peace and welfare.

May we remember, O Father, in all our living together, that righteousness exalteth a nation, and that unless the Lord builds the city, they labor in vain that built it. Amen.

Week 28—Day 6   **Read II Cor. 9:13-15**

A notable European historian has said, "The deed of which the history is told must vibrate in the soul of the historian." The relation of that saying to us is this: as disciples of Christ our commission is to tell the world the deed of God in Christ. If our witness is to have any power and persuasion that deed must vibrate in our own souls.

We thank thee, O God, for thy unspeakable gift in Christ. May we receive that gift with joy that we may tell of it with power. In Jesus' name. Amen.

Week 28—Day 7   **Read Mark 16:15**

We are all familiar with the phrase, "magnificent distance." It comes from the descriptions of Washington, D. C., in the early days as a "city of magnificent distances." It still is, for that matter.

Think of some other "magnificent distances." There is one truly magnificent distance pictured in Mark 16:15. "Go ye

137

into all the world, and preach the gospel to every creature." A long distance to go, but what truly magnificent distances disciples of Christ have gone, against every barrier, into all the world. Here is the same in another form, "unto the uttermost part of the earth" (Acts 1:8). Any distance we travel, whether across the ocean or across the street, with the word and ministry of Christ is a "magnificent distance" in God's sight.

May we truly be messengers of thine, O God, wherever we may go. In Jesus' name. Amen.

Good in the Small Parts

Week 29—Day 1   **Read Matt. 25:24-28**

A very unusual tribute was paid to a British actor, Charles Brookfield, when a critic wrote of him: "He was never a great actor, but he was good in the small parts." Wouldn't most of us settle for that? We have little chance to play the star parts in life's drama. But how much it counts if one is "good in the small parts," the quiet fidelity to tasks, the alert helpfulness to persons in need of any kind of help, the patience given to one's friends and family, the subordination of clamorous self!

O God, help us, instead of complaining that we have only a a small part, to be good in that part. Amen.

Week 29—Day 2   **Read Eph. 4:13-15**

Every tree and bush and plant needs roots to give it "growing points." The tip of the root pushes out and takes in nourishment which enables the plant and tree to grow. Without these growing points pushing out to new sources of sustaining nourishment, life would cease.

We all need "growing points" in our religious life. It is where we push out into active contact with human need of some sort that we find "growing points" for our faith. Belief without doing anything to express that belief in action soon becomes a dead thing.

O God, may our knowledge of thee grow more and more as the days go by. May our activity for thee give growing points to our faith. In Jesus' name. Amen.

Week 29—Day 3   Read Rom. 15:1-3

When Sir Phillip Sidney, one of the noblest men of the age of Queen Elizabeth I, was twelve years old, someone asked him what he was going to do. He replied, "If there are any good wars, I will go to them." We know that there are no good wars in the sense in which young Phillip Sidney used the words. A war with today's weapons can ruin the earth. The "good wars" worth going to are those fought for the blessing of humanity against evil of all sorts, the wars against disease, ignorance, irreligion. Go to those "wars"!

May we be followers of our Master, Christ, and strive to bring deliverance to all who are afflicted and to carry the good news of the gospel. Amen.

Week 29—Day 4   Read Matt: 9:18-21

A college teacher, writing to a friend, complained that he did not get time for all the things he wished to do. "Life here," he wrote, "consists mainly of interruptions." Most of us have had that feeling. Some interruptions are indeed fruitless, but remember that what seem to be tiresome interruptions are often the finest opportunities for service. Go through the Gospels sometime and notice how often Jesus was interrupted. He starts for one place, as in our scripture selection today, and someone in need interrupts him. Some of Jesus' greatest acts of service came through interruptions. It is often so with us.

Keep us, O God, from ever becoming so busy that we cannot stop to reach a helping hand or say a heartening word to one in need. So may we show the spirit of our Lord and Master. Amen.

Week 29—Day 5   **Read Job. 29:13-16**

          In the verses for today Job is listing in his defense what he considers the best things in his life. Note this verse, "I was eyes to the blind and feet to the lame."

Anyone who can say that has made a high use of his life. For that means that his life counted greatly for the welfare of others. He did not go through life with a blindfold over his eyes. How great the need is in our world for *eyes!*

Some have served the blind in physical ways, as did Louis Braille, the Frenchman who invented a system of writing for the blind. Think also of the physicians who have enabled victims of polio to walk again. Think of the opportunities open to us for guidance and support.

Save us, O God, from such self-absorption that we may pass by chances to serve others. Amen.

A woman was greatly embarrassed one night last year when she thought she was taking an aspirin tablet for a headache. She took a pill that brought on sleepiness! Instead of being wide awake and bright at the dinner she attended, she was sleepy.

This mishap raises an important question. Is your religion a sedative or a stimulant? As one wise Christian has said, "If we come to church only to be served, if we come only for rest and relaxation, to acquire peace of mind and to get away from the world and forget all about its problems and needs, we miss the purpose of our religion."

May our faith lead us to service and sacrifice, O God. May our religion be a stimulant and not a sedative. We pray in the spirit of Jesus. Amen.

It is worth noting well what happened after Moses saw the buring bush in the desert. After the high experience of the revelation of God, the command came to Moses, "Go down, Moses, and tell Pharaoh that the Eternal hath said, 'Let my people go.' "

Moses didn't sit around and say, "What a beautiful fire! What color! I will stay here and watch it." No. He heard the word "Go!" and he went. Every fine religious experience is given for a purpose. It is not for us to sit and enjoy it. To us, also, comes the word of God, "Go down into places of need, bring release to all who are bound."

We thank thee, O God, for every revelation of thyself. Grant that all such experiences may quicken us to spend ourselves for others. Amen.

No U Turn

Week 30—Day 1   **Read Acts 9:1-6**

On the parkways and turnpikes of the whole country the sign "No U Turn" is very frequently seen. Of course, it is a good thing to forbid "U turns" for they would badly slow up traffic and cause accidents. But in life, a "U turn" is often the best thing in the world. For it means a "right about face," a turning around from the way one is going, and going the other way. In the Christian life, a vital part of repentance is turning around. Paul made a "U turn" on the Damascus Road. Is there any part of our life about which we should make a right about face?

In every part of our life, O God, may we cease to do evil and learn to do good. In Jesus' name. Amen.

Week 30—Day 2   **Read Col. 1:11**

Jesus said that he had spoken that "your joy might be full." One mark of a Christian ought to be a fullness of joy. Why is it that we do not have the joy that Jesus desired for his disciples? Go over in your mind and ask, what are the things that rob us of joy? Do we allow our fears and worries to depress us? Are we so eager for advancement that the frantic effort to "get on" robs us of joy? Do we allow our prayer life to diminish? Have we allowed our religious life to be too formal a thing?

Each of us will find different answers. Find those which might be keeping you from fullness of joy.

Now may the God of hope fill us with all joy and peace in believing. In Jesus' name. Amen.

Week 30—Day 3   **Read Ps. 51:7-10**

In Thackeray's novel *Vanity Fair* the prinicpal character is Becky Sharp. She makes an excuse for her evil-doing by saying, "I think I could be a good woman if I had five thousand pounds a year." Many people labor under the same delusion. For it *is* a delusion. People say, "If things were different, *I* would be different." We need to free ourselves from all kinds of false excuses, and to confess our sins as being our own fault.

We thank thee, O God, for the assurance that if we confess our sins thou art faithful and just to forgive us our sins and to cleanse us from all unrighteousness. In Jesus' name. Amen.

Week 30—Day 4   **Read II Cor. 6:2**

Think today about the danger of putting off some improvement in our way of living till some future time. James Boswell described his own failure in this regard. He wrote in a letter, "I am always fixing some period for my perfection as far away as possible. Let it be when my account of

Corsica is published. I shall then have a character which I must support." Do you say, "I will do this good thing in the future"?

May we remember, O God, that today is the day of salvation and that thy help is available for us to become better persons this very day. Amen.

Week 30—Day 5   Read Matt. 5:29-30; II Pet. 1:5-7

Stretch your mind a little bit on the matter of putting things into our lives and taking them out. Someone has written about novelists, "Some writers you seem to see hunting about for any significant word they can add. Others are as visibly searching for words to omit."

In living we need to search for both reasons. What can we take out of our lives, such as habits, customs, and employments, to the benefit of the Christian effect of our lives? What can we put into our lives that will add to their usefulness?

We thank thee, O God, for any abilities and powers we have to do good to people. Help us to find the time for doing good. Amen.

Week 30—Day 6   Read Ps. 68:8-10

It is very important to remember that the words in the Psalm, "I shall not be moved," do not mean "my mind is petrified." They mean, "My purpose, my devotion to God, my dedication to him, hold fast."

Many people pride themselves on their inability to be moved

when what happens is that they do not grow. Every thought and idea remain the same as they were in youth. No new understandings of Christ and his work, no enlarged ideas of his kingdom. We know that is wrong. Paul wrote, "Grow up into Christ." "In mind be mature."

Help us, O God, to be steadfast, immovable in our allegiance to thee, always abounding in the work of the Lord. For Jesus' sake. Amen.

Week 30—Day 7   **Read Luke 12:19-21**

In a country churchyard in England there is a tombstone on which are carved the words, under the name of a man, "He died opulent." People who read that are puzzled. The meaning probably is that the man who was buried underneath the tombstone had a good deal of money or property when he died.

Let the words sink into your heart and mind as you read and reread the scripture verses for this day. These words come at the end of Jesus' parable of the rich fool. By financial measurement that man "died opulent" but in a spiritual sense he was a bankrupt. A man may leave a very small estate, but he "dies opulent" if he is rich toward God, if he has the friendship of God, if he is a fellow worker with him, if he has the love of people.

May we always seek first the kingdom of God and his righteousness, and remember that all "these" things will be added. Amen.

WEEK 31

A Great God

Week 31—Day 1　　　　　　　　　**Read Matt. 6:31-33**

　　　　　　A few years ago an author in need of money
—that is a frequent condition with authors—sent a telegram
to his publishers, Simon and Schuster of New York. The telegram read, "How much advance will you give for a novel of
60,000 words?" Mr. Schuster wired back this question, "How
big are the words?"

A good question. For words have a way of shrinking. Take
the word "God," for instance. How big is it to you—not in
general, but in particular, in your own life? Christopher Morley
has said that, to many people, the word "God" is a formula on
Sundays and an oath on week days. Such a God cannot be a
very present help. Our God is a *great* God. How large a place
in each day's thinking does he have with us?

*Deliver us, O God, from the sin of having the wrong pro-
portion in life. May our small concerns not hide from view thy
eternal laws and thy eternal love. Amen.*

Week 31—Day 2　　　　　　　　　**Read Ps. 139:1-6**

　　　　　　A little boy was going with his father up to
the top of the Empire State Building in New York City. The
express elevator shot up with a speed that was literally breath-

taking. When the elevator zooming past the seventy-fifth floor, the boy said to his father, "Does God know we are coming?"

We smile at that, but it does give an opening for a profound truth of our Christian faith. God *does know* all about us. We do not slip out of his mind or notice. "He knoweth the way that we take." "He knoweth our frame." That is a great truth to lean your heart and mind up against. Try it!

O God, there is not a thought in our hearts, but that thou knowest it altogether. Teach us to rely on thy knowledge of us and thy love to us. Amen.

Week 31—Day 3   **Read Rom. 15:13**

We are all familiar with George Frederic Watts' great painting of Hope. A British minister has said that he considers that painting singularly inappropriate. The portrait is that of a woman with a blindfold, striking the one string left on her harp. That is no true representation of Christian hope, for hope is not blind, and it is not despondent. The point seems to be well taken. For to have hope in a bad situation, or a bad world, is to rely on the inexhaustible resources of God, and the love of God.

May the God of hope fill us with all joy and peace in believing. In Jesus' name. Amen.

Week 31—Day 4   **Read 11 Cor. 1:20-22**

An article in the *New York Times* was headed, "New Age of Promise Ahead." It declared the promises and "sweeping changes of the last decade have made our great country more than ever the land of opportunity." The author dismisses all fear of a recurring depression. Everything, according to him, is getting "bigger and better." He cites the engineering marvels, the new suburban developments, new advances in every field.

For all of this we may be and should be grateful. Yet we should not bank too heavily on greater machines for true welfare. Man makes promises. But the real reliance for mankind is in the promises of God. The promises of God, such as "Blessed is the nation whose god is the Lord," are better than the promises of guided missiles, satellites, and hydrogen bombs.

Teach us to remember that righteousness exalteth a nation. In Jesus' name. Amen.

Week 31—Day 5   **Read I Cor. 9:24-26**

Read carefully these words from *Walden* by Henry D. Thoreau, and then think of the last few words of it.

"I went to the woods because I wished to live deliberately, to front only the essential facts of life, and see if I could learn what it had to teach, and not, when I came to die, discover that I had not lived."

It would be a shock to learn at the end of life that we "had not lived." But we will come to such a discovery, that we have missed life in its highest sense, "the life which is life indeed," if we have not had the high experience of knowing God through Jesus Christ and becoming his disciple. That is the highest prize that life has to offer.

150

We thank thee, O God, that thou has ever called us out of our darkness. May we walk in the light as thou dost give us light. Amen.

Week 31—Day 6   **Read Phil. 4:10-13**

In John Stuart Mill's autobiography, he tells of his unusual education. He was a very precocious child. His father educated the boy himself and literally crammed the head of his young son with knowledge. But James Mill, the father, had no religious faith and would not allow any religion to be taught the boy. Many years later when John Stuart Mill was a famous man, he looked back on his education with a great sense of loss. His mind was stuffed with information; his soul was starved. He said, "I was left at the commencement of my voyage with a well-equipped ship and a rudder but no sail." That figure of speech is worth stopping to consider. A ship needs more than a rudder if it is to get anywhere. It needs a sail to connect with the power! A life needs a rudder, for it needs direction. It needs to know what is right. But it needs power to do right. It needs the driving power of a real faith in God and love of God.

We thank thee, O God, for the gift of Jesus Christ, through whom we may be more than conquerors over evil and weakness. Amen.

Week 31—Day 7   **Read Matt. 10:37-39**

There is a fine sentence by James Reid of England which is worth engraving on the mind. It expresses

151

a great truth of wide application. He wrote, "The secret of a fresh interest in life does not lie merely in fresh scenes. It lies in the recovery of the sense of God's purpose for us." How many people try vainly to get a fresh interest in life by traveling from place to place like delirious grasshoppers. But, as was said of one of these travelers, "Poor old Jones, he has to take himself with him wherever he goes." Many marriages have failed, not because the partners did not love each other at the beginning, but because they never lifted their love up to the clear light of God's purpose for them.

We thank thee, O God, that thou dost have a purpose for our lives. May we seek earnestly to keep them in line with thy purposes. Amen.

WEEK 32

A Lonesome Drum

Week 32—Day 1   **Read Ps. 26:8-11**

In the midst of busy days and various pulls in all directions, it is well to remember the words of Henry Thoreau on the high duty of keeping our minds open to the highest call. He said that often when a person is out of step with his neighbors it is because "he hears a different drummer." It is possible to be out of step with a large company of people around us because we do not follow the orders of the crowd but we "hear a different drummer," even Jesus. Listen for a lonesome drum!

Remind us, O God, of our citizenship in the Eternal City, and make us responsive to a higher wisdom than that of earth, even the wisdom of Jesus Christ. Amen.

Week 32—Day 2   **Read II Cor. 6:1-2**

Here is a word from the scientist, Madame Marie Curie, which should be remembered by all who tend to put off the joy of their religion and its service to some future date. She wrote once to her children, "I send you my best wishes for a year in which you will have pleasure in living every day without waiting for the days to be gone before finding charm in them, and without putting all hope of pleasure in the days to come."

This plea applies to our spiritual life. The first word of Jesus' recorded ministry included the word "today." We are told, "Now is the day of salvation." Jesus' answer to everyone who said "Suffer me first" was "now." Do not put off trust in God or service to God to any tomorrow.

May we give ourselves, O God, to thy service now, and have now the joy of the Lord. Amen.

Week 32—Day 3 — Read II Tim. 3:3-5

A historian, talking to some children in school, said, "Remember, it is not what you give to a person that makes him love you, but what you ask him to give of himself."

That may not seem to be true at first glance. But if you think it over you will see that it is true. Our love to a parent is not so much for lavish gifts, but for the way in which they hold us up to our best. We are grateful for the "hard" teacher, who made us give of ourselves in work. We are grateful for the "hard" command of Christ, "Take up your cross and follow me." For only in that way can we become Christlike.

O God, may we not only listen to thy word but follow Thee. Amen.

Week 32—Day 4 — Read Jas. 1:27; I. John 3:17-18

A great many people have read the book by Clarence Day, Jr., entitled *Life With Father*. He records

154

one thing about his father's attitude to worship which should start us thinking about our own religious attitudes and our work for the church and kingdom of God. "When my father went to church and sat in his pew, he felt he was doing enough and further spiritual work ought to be done by the clergy." Do we think as Day did? Or do we think we owe more to God than to sit in our pew, as though we were doing him a favor?

May our service to Thee, O God, be not a grudging minimum, but may we give thee of our time and strength in full measure. In Jesus' name. Amen.

Week 32—Day 5   **Read Rev. 3:14-16**

     Samuel Butler, the novelist, made a very bitter and cynical remark when he said, "The best way to lay the ghost of Jesus Christ is to be a moderate churchman."

We could amend that and say—one sure way to weaken the influence of Jesus Christ in the world is to be a very moderate churchman. That will mean that we do not believe too strongly, do not care too much, or work too hard. Such indifferent "moderation" will never persuade anyone to believe in Christ or to work for him.

Help us, O God, to be fellow workers with God, and to love and serve him, not moderately, but tremendously. Amen.

Week 32—Day 6   **Read John 13:34-35**

     Samuel Johnson once said of Joseph Addison's poetry, "He thinks justly, but he thinks faintly." Carry

155

that judgment over into religious life and see how closely—
and disturbingly—it applies. So many people think "justly"
and truly in their conception of the gospel. They know what
the Christian revelation is. But it is all so faint. It doesn't seem
to stand out in their lives like a sign printed with large black
letters. It doesn't seem to make much difference. They know
the words, "Take up your cross and follow me." But it is faint.

*Help us, O God, to make our discipleship so clear that it is
never in doubt. Amen.*

Week 32—Day 7   **Read Ps. 91:1-5**

Note one word particularly in this psalm,
"dwelleth." That does not mean visit. There is a vast difference
between *visiting* a place and *living* in it. So there is a vast difference between living in the secret place of communion with
God, having it as the background of all your life, and "dropping
in occasionally." Do we live in God's love, or just drop in now
and then? Read the whole 91st psalm. What a place to live!

*O God, help us to make the Lord ever the Most High, our
refuge and habitation.*

WEEK 33

The Muted Trumpet

Week 33—Day 1   **Read Matt. 6:1-4**

A wonderful plea against "blowing our own trumpets" is in the sixth chapter of Matthew. That plea is, in effect, "Put a mute on the wind instruments." We all have a problem in how to deal with the trumpets and big horns of self-interest and self-advertisement. We all have trumpets, announcing in firm tones, "This is I. Better pay attention." The trumpet makes good music—in an orchestra when it is mixed in with other instruments. All by itself it can be a terrible blare! A man said of a friend, "He has I-ritis," meaning that he keeps saying "I" all the time. We need to make a persistent effort to put a mute on the wind instruments. Here is the high goal set by Jesus, "Do not sound a trumpet before you that you may have glory of men."

Wilt thou, O God, increase in our lives, that we may decrease. May we always live so that men may glorify God. Amen.

Week 33—Day 2   **Read Rom. 12:2-3**

When Henry Thoreau, the author of "Walden," was about eight years old, a visitor in the home asked him the familiar question, "What are you going to be when you grow up?" Young Thoreau replied quite solemnly, "I'll be

157

I." No one ever lived up to that high program better than did Thoreau! He maintained a stout individuality all of his life. He never just "went along with the crowd."

Another notable New England literary figure who lived during the first part of the last century was Margaret Fuller. Emerson said of her, "She had a mountainous me." That sounds like what young Thoreau said, but it is very different. The "I'll be I" meant that Thoreau would never be a frightened conformist. The "mountainous me" meant that Miss Fuller was self-insistent, wanting her own way and her place in everything. Sometimes, to hear her was like hearing a singer practicing and saying over and over, "Mi, mi, mi, mi."

Grant, O God, that in us, Christ may increase, and that our selfish demands on life may decrease. Amen.

Week 33—Day 3   **Read Phil. 3:12-14**

A little girl had come home from her first day at school. Her father, teasing her a bit, asked, "Well, did you learn everything today?" "No," she answered with disappointment. "I have to go back tomorrow." It is a blessed thing to realize that we have not learned everything and that we have to go back tomorrow and tomorrow. Let us keep humility in our hearts and minds and make life a long experience in learning wonderful things out of God's law and out of God's world.

May we press on, O God, to the mark of our high calling in Christ Jesus, ever seeking to know more of thee and to become more effective workers for thee. In the name of him we serve, Jesus Christ. Amen.

William Allen White tells of a friend of his, a Kansas architect, who spent several days looking carefully at the Chartres Cathedral, studying it with wonder, both outside and inside. Then he said, "I am going to study architecture." He was already an architect, rated a very successful one. But when he had seen the glories of that cathedral, he realized how much more there was for him to learn.

A service much like that is done for us by great persons living and dead. This greatness takes away all our self-satisfaction. Let us keep great souls living in our minds and memories.

Help us, O God, to respond to the best and highest when we see it in human lives. Amen.

Saint Augustine once made a prayer which has become well-known. He prayed, "Lord, save me from that evil man—myself!" Compare to that the prayer of an early Wesleyan preacher in England, James Spence: "Lord, save me from that good man, James Spence." Both prayers had real insight and knowledge of life. For we need to be saved, not only from our evil self, but from our *good* self. For often men go wrong through complacency and self-satisfaction. When we feel ourselves to be "good," we are in danger, for then we are in great spiritual danger of pride and self-satisfaction. When we are tempted to admire ourselves, then we need God's grace to be saved and to keep the humility without which we cannot be true Christians. Jesus pointed out that subtle danger in his parable of the Pharisee and the Publican. The Pharisee needed to be saved from that "good" man—himself!

Preserve in us, O God, true humility, and save us from all self-righteousness. Remind us to pray every day, "God be merciful to me, a sinner." Amen.

Week 33—Day 6　　　　　　　　**Read Luke 12:27-32**

A good example of a complacent sort of religion which regards God as a kind of high-class servant who can be used to get what a person wants, is found in a familiar story by Dorothy Parker, entitled "Wonderful Old Gentleman." She writes about a woman in the story: "Mrs. Whittaker's tolerance was not confined to her less fortunate relatives. It extended to God who had always supplied her with the best service. She could have given Him an excellent reference at any time." That cuts sharply!

"That doesn't touch me. I do not have a patronizing idea of God." Of course not! Yet do we have the true attitude which ought to mark our conception of God and our relation to him? That right attitude is seen in two instances in the Bible, among many. There is the passage when Isaiah gets a vision of God and it makes him say, "I am a man of unclean lips." Peter sees Jesus and says, "Depart from me, O Lord, for I am a sinful man."

Grant unto us, O God, the spirit of humility. Deepen within us the sense of our own unworthiness. Amen.

"What manner of communications are these that you have one to another . . ?" Jesus asks the disciples walking to Emmaus after the crucifixion. Earlier, as recorded in Mark, Jesus asks his disciples the same question, "What was it that ye disputed among yourselves . . ?" It was embarrassing in the latter case, because they were discussing who should be greatest. What a frequent subject that is with us—"Who shall be greatest"! We feel, even if we do not say, "I am as great as he is; I ought to have first place." How would we like to have Jesus join our company and ask, "What were you talking about?" God *does know.*

May our conversations and our inmost desires be such that we can always welcome thee to join them. Amen.

WEEK 34

Deadline

There is an imaginary line which looms large in the thinking of many people called the "deadline." It is supposed to be an age limit at which a person is no longer effective. Fortunately, ideas on that subject are changing. We are coming to see that no age limit bars a person's effectiveness.

There is a deadline which is very real, however, and which we should watch for carefully. Someone said truly, "A deadline is where something dies." We reach a deadline in our spiritual life when we cease to grow, when we are deadened by routines, when we grow complacent and self-satisfied.

Help us, O God, to choose life. Amen.

Someone has pointed out the strikingly different use of the same words in the Genesis story of the building of the tower of Babel, and the story of the call of Abraham. Those who, in their pride, started to build the tower of Babel said, "Let us make us a name." Then, later, in the twelfth chapter God said to Abraham, "I will bless thee and make thy name great." Many people today say to themselves, "I will make me a great name." So, ambition and the desire for wealth and power push them along. Others strive to let God make them great. They do not seek great things for themselves, but they strive that they may attain true greatness as servants of God. What kind of name do we seek, that which comes from pride and power, or that which comes from obedience to God?

O thou great Friend of all the sons of men, may we be to others what thou art to us, strength in time of need. Amen.

Week 34—Day 3   Read Matt. 12:35-37

We read in the twelfth chapter of Matthew that we will be called into judgment for "every idle word." That is a sobering statement, for the Christian control of the tongue is a demanding task. So much damage is caused by idle, thoughtless, irresponsible words. "Idle" words are not light, pleasant, good natured small talk. There is a blessed place for that in our lives. "Idle words" in the sense the term is used in this chapter are those words which cause damage by untruth, or by malicious spirit.

But it is also true that we will be called into judgment for *every busy silence*. We are guilty of a "busy silence" when the time for a clear witness to Christ has come, and we are too busy to speak that word. We are guilty of a "busy silence" when a word of encouragement, of sympathy and comfort might be given to someone in need, and we are too busy to speak that word.

Help us, O God, to obey the injunction, "Let the redeemed of the Lord say so." May we be ready to witness to our Lord and Master. Amen.

A musical direction which accompanies a hymn in one of our widely used hymnbooks is quite suggestive. Under the title is given this information: "For an easier key, see Number 336." That is all. But it does suggest many things. Very often people desire to put the commandments of God and the words of Jesus to "an easier key." The stern command of God, for instance, "Thou shalt not covet," is difficult. The words of Christ, "Take up your cross and follow me," is demanding. So many people say, "Let's put it in an easier key." And they do. Instead of saying, "All men are brothers," which would cause them to change their habits, they put God's love in an "easier key" and make the circle of their care and concern limited to their own color and class, and nation. How about us?

Help us, O God, not to weaken thy words to suit our own weakness. Help us with thy strength to do thy will. Amen.

One problem we all have in trying to live moral and religious lives is that of self-correction. James McNeil Whistler, the artist, said a memorable word about self-correction in painting. He once wiped a canvas clean, after spending many hours on it, saying, "It is not good enough." A friend said, "Well, why not wait till morning to wipe it off?" "No," said Mr. Whistler. "If I left it till tomorrow, I might have persuaded myself it was good enough to leave permanently." He did not trust himself, lest he think, "This is good enough."

Save us, O God, from the temptation of thinking that careless, thoughtless conduct on our part is good enough to offer thee. Help us always to give and to be our best. Amen.

The finest tribute possible to actors in a Shakespearean play was paid by a critic to *Romeo and Juliet* as played many years ago by Leslie Howard and Norma Shearer. He wrote, simply, "Shakespeare would have liked it." There can be no greater satisfaction in anything we can do than the honest feeling, "Jesus would have liked it." There is no reward on earth to compare with that.

May we seek thy approval, O God, in everything that we do, and seek it more eagerly than approval from any other. Amen.

We talk much about our "busy lives." How busy is "too busy"? A publisher wrote this bit of good sense the other day: "Somehow the old 'too busy' excuse doesn't sound so convincing as it used to. I've seen too many people who were too busy doing nothing to donate their time to doing something. Also, I have seen some people who seem to be overloaded with work, who never seem 'too busy' to take on something extra for a good cause."

If we are "too busy" to worship God, to give time to our families, to take responsibility for the welfare of our community, we are altogether too busy.

Help us, O God, to divide our time rightly, that things which matter most in our lives and the life of the world may have a rightful share of our time and strength. Amen.

A Daily Beauty

Week 35—Day 1   **Read Luke 15:21**

There is a wonderful thing which Iago says about Cassio in Shakespeare's play, *Othello*. He says, "He hath a daily beauty in his life that makes me ugly." That, magnified many, many times is what Jesus makes us think of ourselves. Peter felt that way when he saw Jesus by the lakeside. He said, "Depart from me, O Lord, for I am a sinful man." He has truly a "daily beauty in his life" that makes us ugly. Look at him often, in the pages of the Gospels. The beauty in his life will save us from self-satisfaction and will lead us to repentance.

Help us, O God, to see ourselves as we really are, ugly, compared to the beauty of our Master. May we strive to become more like Jesus. Amen.

Week 35—Day 2   **Read Luke 21:32-33**

A great violinist, Isaac Stern, was being congratulated on his brilliant playing of a Beethoven concerto. Modestly, he gave the credit to Beethoven. "You can work on a Beethoven concerto for fifty years and never find a final answer. It is capable of any kind of expression and new ideas. It is an alive thing."

A beautiful tribute to great music. The history of Christ in the Gospels is also "an alive thing." We can never capture all of Christ's meaning. He finds new expressions in each new generation. The joy and wonder of the story is that a lifetime of study, and meditation brings out new meanings.

May we be faithful, O God, in keeping thy truth before our eyes and imaginations, that we may behold wondrous things out of thy law. Amen.

Week 35—Day 3   **Read Matt. 16:13-17**

Lewis Carroll, the author of *Alice in Wonderland,* wrote a little fantasy about a lock which kept running around in distress, crying, "I'm looking for someone to unlock me." The little story is so strange as to sound ridiculous. Yet that is a picture to hold in mind. For many people need a key to unlock them. They need an influence in their lives which will bring out their powers locked within them. Often danger, or the need to help others, brings out unsuspected powers. Think of the way in which Jesus "unlocked" people. Peter, for instance, in the companionship of Jesus, had his powers of strength and daring brought out. Our hidden powers may be "unlocked" if we allow Christ to come into our lives.

May there be room in our hearts and lives, O God, for thee. Amen.

Week 35—Day 4   **Read Gal. 2:20**

Ralph Waldo Emerson once said, "Hold a straw parallel to the Gulf Stream and the Atlantic Ocean will flow through it." That is true. You can prove it!

167

Here is something else true. Hold your life parallel to the life of Christ and the power of God will flow through it. That is true. You can prove it.

Out of our weakness, O God, may we be made strong by opening our minds and hearts to thy Grace. Amen.

Week 35—Day 5 **Read Luke 5:6-8**

Lady Mary Wortley Montague, a notable society leader and writer in London in the eighteenth century, in her later years went eleven years without looking in a mirror. She said that she found her face disagreeable and so never looked at it again! Quite an achievement for a woman!

Consider the need of every person to look in some kind of mirror. The greatest "mirror" for showing us what we are is Jesus Christ. Of course, as we look at him we do not see our exact likeness, but we do see our smallness against his greatness, our selfishness compared to his love, our cowardice against his courage.

We thank thee, O God, for Jesus Christ. May we look often at him and be saved from any self-satisfaction. Amen.

Week 35—Day 6 **Read Luke 24:13-31**

In the beautiful story of the walk to Emmaus after the resurrection, a walk on which the risen Lord joined the two disciples, note one sentence which fits into our journeys of every sort every day. It is, "While they communed together and reasoned, Jesus himself drew near."

Pray that that may happen every day. We spend a large part of our day talking and discussing, communing and reasoning. That is inevitable and right. How else could we do our work or live our lives fully? But let us include Jesus in our remembrance and remember that beyond our thought is God's better thought.

May we not get so far from thy purposes, O God, that Jesus himself may not draw near to us. For Jesus' sake. Amen.

Week 35—Day 7   **Read John 1:40-42**

Robert Louis Stevenson, when a young man making his first endeavors as an author, wrote, "There is something in me worth saying, though I can't find what it is just yet." Keep that sentence in mind, and meditate on the service which Christ, through our faith in him, performs for us. He helps us to find and bring to use our best possibilities. He discovered and brought to light the unknown powers in Peter, in Paul, in Augustine, and in a great host of his disciples, living and dead.

Help us, O God, to place in thy hands all our talents and possibilities and allow thee to shape us for thy purposes. In Jesus' name. Amen.

Far Horizons

Week 36—Day 1   **Read Isa. 33:17**

One of the most serious losses of life in a big city is the absence of horizons. If this seems exaggerated, try it on yourself. Those who live in cities can testify that in crowded streets it is impossible to see a sunset or a sunrise. It is impossible to see over the buildings. In the midst of high buildings life is like living in a narrow gorge. There is a real loss of horizons.

That is the great calamity in life of our mind and spirit, the loss of horizons. Christian faith gives us far horizons—the horizon of eternity which surrounds our life in time, the horizon of God who is the background of our material life.

May we daily lift our eyes, O God, to the hills and remember our help cometh from the Lord. Amen.

Week 36—Day 2   **Read Matt. 20:25-28**

There are several meanings to the phrase, "extending yourself." It may mean "doing your utmost," "putting all your strength into an endeavor." It may mean "swelling up with your own importance." A person who "struts" in a vainglorious, exhibitionist manner tries to "extend himself" and make himself seem important.

There is a higher way of extending yourself than that. You can "extend yourself" beyond the narrow one-room cell of your own interest and advantage into other lives. We can by our interest in Christian churches overseas, extend ourselves and our influence around the globe. That is a lot better than just living in our own back yard.

Help us, O God, to answer thy invitation to go into all the world and preach the gospel. Amen.

Week 36—Day 3   Read Jas. 1:27

A novel of a few years ago had this description of a man, the head of a large business: "Like most men of his sort, he was all concern and genuine kindness when he was immediately faced with distress, when it was a matter of quick, short range sympathy."

That raises the question for us to answer, "How far does our sympathy reach?" Are the things which stir you to active sympathy just the things that happen in front of your eyes? Or can you respond to a need that may be a long distance from you? Christ said, "into all the world."

Help us to remember, O God, that whatever we do to anyone, across the street or across the sea, we do it unto Christ. In his name. Amen.

Week 36—Day 4   Read Rom. 12:15

Here is a beautiful story of Abraham Lincoln, showing the wide range of his sympathy with others. Two women relatives of General Lew Wallace sought news at the White House after a battle. After learning that Wallace was safe, they spoke glibly of their gladness that one casualty

171

was "not our Wallace." Lincoln's rebuke took the form of mournfully meditating aloud, "It was somebody's Wallace, wasn't it?"

It is a good thing to remember always the sorrow that comes to "somebody." This prevents our being locked up in our own affairs and keeps our sympathies warm.

Save us, O God, from ourselves, for we can be our own worst enemies when we become self-absorbed. Amen.

Week 36—Day 5   **Read Matt. 9:36-38**

A man walked up behind a friend and suddenly spoke to him in a loud voice. The friend said, "My, you made me jump out of my skin." The man replied, "That might be a good thing."

Truly, it would be a good thing for all of us, to be able to jump out of our skins more often. General Charles Gordon used to speak of "the sovereign duty of crawling under the other man's skin." We ought to get out of our own skin and put ourselves, in dedicated imagination, into the situation of other people, to know how the man with a dark skin feels under many discriminations. We need to feel with and for other people.

Teach us, O God, to have quick and understanding compassion for all who are in any kind of need. Amen.

Week 36—Day 6   **Read Matt. 28:18-20**

During the Second World War, the managing editor of the Brooklyn, N. Y., *Eagle* kept on his desk a sign which read, "Always remember that a dog fight in Brooklyn is more important than a revolution in China." That was a lie! Now we have learned that a revolution in China results in funerals in Brooklyn, and funerals are more important than dog fights. Today foreign news is local news. Foreign news is no farther away than the local draft board. "The man about town must become the man about planet." The Christian must, in his thinking and his acting, follow the commandment of Jesus and go into all the world.

Help us, O God of all men, to enlarge the dimensions of our minds and hearts. May nothing that concerns men and women, our brothers and sisters in Christ, be foreign to us. Amen.

Week 36—Day 7   **Read Eccl. 2:14**

Henry D. Thoreau, the author of *Walden*, said, "I have traveled much in Concord." That was true. He spent most of his life in the little town of Concord, Mass., but he really *saw* more of the world, more of nature, and more of people than many who go back and forth across the ocean and around the globe. Some of these people never depart from the narrow circle of themselves.

You can "travel much" in the spot where you live. If you keep your mind and heart open, you can see the world with a fresh wonder, you can see people, not as objects in the landscape but as people to be known and loved and served. Do not travel blind.

Open our eyes, O God, that we may see wondrous things out of thy law, and out of thy world and children. Amen.

A Land Where the
Great Streams Rise

Week 37—Day 1   **Read Mark 5:18-19**

A Scottish minister once paid a beautiful tribute to his native country, the highlands of Scotland. He said, "It is a land where the great streams rise." That was not only poetic but true. From highland lakes, often covered with mist, flow down streams which turn the wheels that give light, heat, and power to great cities such as Glasgow and Edinburgh.

The same is true of religious experience. There is a sort of mist about the spirit of God in our life, but from that relationship there flow streams of energy and power and blessedness into the world.

Out of the grace which we receive from thee, O God, enable us to give forth helpful service to our fellows. Amen.

Week 37—Day 2   **Read Matt. 25:14-17**

A woman in a city in Connecticut discovered some time ago that her money, left to her by inheritance, had been depleted by a careless trustee, because he did not provide for investment. The capital diminished by his refusal to allow it to be spent. In the parable of the talents Jesus stresses the necessity of investment. That applies to our spiritual inherit-

174

ance as well as to money. If our faith is not to ooze away, it must be renewed and invested in enterprises of the kingdom of God.

Grant, O God, that we may be faithful stewards of all that has been committed to us. Amen.

Week 37—Day 3   **Read Mark 6:30-32**

We read in the early history of Massachusetts of a strange form of execution. The victims of the hysteria about witchcraft in Salem where all hanged except one. He was "pressed to death." We do not know just what horrible, cruel form of death that was. In some way pressure was applied which caused the breath and heart to stop. The phrase is provocative when thought of in connection with the spiritual life. We can be so busy with many concerns, running here, there, and everywhere, with no room for quiet, prayer or meditation, that our inner, spiritual life is overwhelmed. It is "pressed to death."

Help us, O God, to make a place for the preservation of our inner life. Amen.

Week 37—Day 4   **Read Luke 24:30-32**

Some of you have known a mountain. You know well you never get all of a mountain in a day, or a month, or a year. How ridiculous it would be for a person to say, "I know Pikes Peak. I saw it through a car window." One cannot really see Pikes Peak through a car window. A mountain does not disclose all its secrets, its varying moods, its different scenes to a hasty tourist.

175

It is just the same with the great passages of Scripture. No one snares the meaning of the truths of the Bible in a hasty glance. It takes years of living with them. Only by such thoughtful study do we really know them.

May we patiently give larger and larger entrance to thy word, that we may walk in the light. Amen.

Week 37—Day 5   **Read Isa. 40:29-31**

A scholar doing some research on the Puritans of New England came upon the roll of a church. There were many strange names, such as Stand-Fast-in-the-Faith Brown, and Hope-in-Mercy Martin. The scholar said that he had no desire to have such a name. But he came across one name which he said he wished might have been a description of him! Renewed Robinson. "That is what I need," he said, "to be renewed." Don't we all? One of the joyful, heartening things about our religion is that we may be renewed. By God's grace we can all have a life made over. Take into your mind and heart such great pictures of God's renewal as "He restoreth my soul," and "They that wait upon the Lord shall renew their strength."

O God, when we get tired and our strength is worn down, may we come to thee for renewal so that we may run and not be weary and walk and not faint. Amen.

Week 37—Day 6   **Read Matt. 17:22-23**

In today's scripture reading Jesus tells his disciples of his coming death and resurrection. Then follows
176

the words, "They were exceedingly sorry." It was natural that they should be sorry for his predicted suffering and death. But apparently they paid no attention to the announcement of his resurrection. They concentrated on his death as though that were all. We are often like the disciples in that. We pay far too little attention to the resurrection of Christ. We often act, in thinking of life and death, as though the resurrection had never happened. We do not allow it to have the tremendous meaning for our lives that it should have. Looking unto Jesus, who died and rose again, we should not be always exceedingly sorry but exceedingly joyful.

We thank thee, O God, for the victory of Christ over sin and death. May we who are risen with Christ seek those things that are above. Amen.

Week 37—Day 7   **Read Gal. 6:8-10**

A man who goes about town sharpening scissors and knives has this sign stamped on his wagon, "Every thing sharpened that needs an edge." We all know how quickly kitchen knives which we use every day need an edge. The same is true of our goodness. It gets dull. Our goodness needs an edge, that it may not be just conventional goodness, but warm, outgoing, self-forgetful love, exceeding the "righteousness of the scribes and Pharisees."

We pray thee, O God, that we may give of ourselves unreservedly. In the name of him who gave his life a ransom for many. Amen.

WEEK 38

Never Lower the Flag

Week 38—Day 1   **Read II Tim. 4:6-8**

In a tribute to a woman, a friend wrote discerningly, "She kept her vision and tenacity of character. Her life was exhausting, but she stayed on the course and never lowered the flag." Could a person win a finer tribute than that? How much greater an achievement in real living than any material success is the record, "She never lowerd her flag." That is the high tribute which, with God's help, we may win and deserve. That tribute is practically the same which Paul humbly claimed, as found in our scripture reading for today.

Grant, O God, that having enrolled as thy disciples, we may keep the faith and finish the course. Amen.

Week 38—Day 2   **Read Luke 12:4-7**

Men have always sought security, but our times have given a new urgency to the old quest. Men seek security on every hand, with social security, pensions, job tenure, savings. The way in which this has been elevated to be a national idol is found in a recent advertisement which read: "All our adventures begin and come home to the security we cannot do without. To give and get security is the main business of living. It provides us life's finest rewards." The gospel of Christ urges us to seek "security," but it directs our endeavor in other directions than that of piling up financial strength. It points to the true security in God. That security is sure, both in this world and the next. Faith sings, "A mighty fortress is our God, a bulwark never failing."

Lead us, O God, to seek the meaning of life, not in the abundance of things, but in the abundance of thy love and care. Amen.

Week 38—Day 3   **Read Acts 4:13-20**

Here is a good sentence to remember in these days, when the pressures upon us to be conformed to the ways of the world are so great and constant. Robert Louis Stevenson wrote, "To do anything not because the thing is good or kind or honest in its own right but because others are doing it, is to resign all moral control and captaincy upon yourself, and go post haste to the devil with the greatest number."

The opposite to that surrender is expressed in the words of Peter to the high priest, "We must obey God rather than man."

Give us the courage, O God, to stand for the best we have learned from Christ and not to follow a multitude away from him. Amen.

Week 38—Day 4   **Read Ps. 44:17-21**

Some modern translations of the Bible give us a word worth keeping in mind by every Christian. It is the word "flinch." The dictionary gives the meaning as "to shrink back or recoil from fear or danger." Moffatt translates the verse about Moses in the book of Hebrews, "Like one who saw the

179

King invisible, he never flinched" (Heb. 11:27-28). The other use of the word is in Ps. 44:18, "our heart has never flinched." We can be equipped to keep from flinching in the presence of some duty or opportunity for service, by the same means that fortified Moses, by seeing the God who is invisible and being grounded in him.

May we remember, O God, that faith is the victory over life's temptations and obstacles. Amen.

Week 38—Day 5   **Read Num. 13:26-31**

The story of the spies sent into the promised land of Canaan is enormously important for many reasons. One reason is that it comes so close to life. When we face things difficult or too hard for us, it is common to say, "We can't do it." That is very often the attitude of the majority. But there is also a minority which says like Caleb, "We are able. We can do it." Oliver Wendell Holmes says of such situations, "When a resolute young fellow steps up to the great bully, the world, and takes him boldly by the beard, he is often surprised to find that it comes off in his hand, and that it was only tied on to scare timid adventurers." Step up to evil in God's name and with his help!

Deliver us from fear, O God. Make us strong in thy might for all thou dost ask us to do. Amen.

Week 38—Day 6   **Read Luke 15:31-33**

Alan Paton, who has inspired many in different countries by his deeply religious novel *Cry, the Beloved*
180

Country was speaking lately of the need for Christian effort amid bad social conditions. He said, "If we wait till the time is ripe, we may wait till it is *rotten*." In other words, if we wait until the time is just right for our effort, we will wait forever. The voices of laziness and cowardice whisper in our ear, "Don't do anything now. The time is not ripe." The time for the early church to go out to the Roman empire with the strange gospel of a man crucified on a cross was not ideal. But it was God's time. Any time to preach the gospel and to put on the whole armour of God in a struggle for righteousness is God's right time.

Save us, O God eternal, from putting off action for thee. May we never forget the word of scripture, "Today is the day of salvation." Amen.

Week 38—Day 7   **Read Is. 41:8-10**

There is a word in common use in the days of England's Queen Elizabeth the First and in the days of the Puritans which is not used any more. It is a good word: "answerable." Queen Elizabeth used it thus, "Though I be a woman, I have as good a courage answerable to my place as ever my father had." Governor Bradford of the Plymouth colony in Massachusetts said the people in the colony had an "answerable courage" to all their trials.

We, too, have trials. May we have "answerable" courage.

May we, O God, be strong, in the Lord and in the power of his might. Amen.

Like One Man

Week 39—Day 1   Read Eph. 4:1-3

It was said in tribute to Arturo Toscanini, the orchestra leader, that "he could make 100 pieces sing like one man."

That is also a beautiful picture of a church in which all the members are held together in devotion to their Master. That, indeed, is the "unity of the spirit in the bond of peace." May our individual devotion to Christ be merged in the common devotion of our church.

Let, O God, the gentle power of Christ become our strength in all we do or endure. In his name. Amen.

Week 39—Day 2   Read Eph. 5:27

In a poetic drama of Anglo-Saxon England, by Edna St. Vincent Millay, there is a magnificent line spoken by the Archbishop of Canterbury. Ours is a time when the difficulties and demands on the church are great. In the play the Archbishop says to those who are threatening to "wipe out" the church, "The Church of God is not a candle, blow on!"

That says to us, "Have faith in God." God is in the midst of his church. He will not fail, and his church will not be "wiped out."

May we, O God, give to thy church our undivided allegiance, not merely a small part of ourselves but all of ourselves, that
182

we may be worthy of the great head of the church, even Jesus Christ. Amen.

Week 39—Day 3 **Read Col. 3:16**

One of the reasons given for the defeat of the Confederate Army at the Battle of Gettysburg is the conduct of General J. E. B. Stuart. He set off two days before the battle on a useless raid and lost contact with the main army and was unable to inform General Lee about the Union Army's plans.

Think of the phrase, "lost contact with the main army." That is a bad thing in any warfare. It is a bad thing in the Christian's battle against evil. We should not lose contact with the host of Jesus' followers, the Church.

We thank thee, O God, for the help we receive from the fellowship of thy Church. Amen.

Week 39—Day 4 **Read Ps. 20:1-5**

An enterprising bookseller, hoping to attract buyers, once displayed over a stack of Bibles a song which read, "Satan trembles when he sees Bibles sold at low as these." Perhaps! Though of course that is not as true as the original words of which those lines are a parody: "Satan trembles when he sees the weakest saint upon his knees." But evidently Satan does *not* tremble just to see the announcement that church service will be held at "11 A.M. as usual." For the words "as usual" may mean "stiff and lifeless." That would not scare anyone. But there is deep truth in the saying of C. S. Lewis, "To see a church with all its banners flying, is enough to make all hell tremble."

May we lift thy banner over us, O God, that thy name and thy kingdom may not suffer loss by our lives. Deliver us from evil. Amen.

Week 39—Day 5   **Read Eph. 5:27**

In Clifford Dowdey's book *Experiment in Rebellion* we read an interesting fact about the religion of Jefferson Davis, the president of the Confederacy. When the Union army in 1862 was within twenty miles of Richmond, Davis was baptized by the rector of St. Paul's Church and received into the church as a member.

Think of it! All the years of his life he never bothered to join the church. But when the Union army got within twenty miles of Richmond, evidently he got scared and hurried to get enrolled in the church! All the years he missed the fellowship of the church, he missed the opportunity to serve in and through the church.

The church is not something to *run to* in times of trouble. It is something to *march with* at all times.

Help us to say all of our days, I love thy church, O God. Amen.

Week 39—Day 6   **Read Isa. 51:9**

In the autobiography of Edward Gibbon, author of the *Decline and Fall of the Roman Empire*, he records a passing regret that he had not been a lawyer or a trades-man, or a civil officer in India, or, even embraced "the fat slumbers of the church." What a horrible phrase, "the fat slumbers of the church"! But that is exactly what many churches had in those years.

When a church slumbers, evil thrives. Do your attitudes and actions keep your church from slumber?

Help us to put first in our lives the things that count most and put other things behind them. Amen.

Week 39—Day 7   **Read Heb. 1:1; John 14:12**

The Christian society is in three parts: those who are living, those who are dead, and those yet to be born. They are all bound together in Christ. The saints who have gone before have left us a great family inheritance. In their faith, their courage, their sacrificial service, we are enriched. To those living we should give our love and our service, for we are all one in Christ Jesus. We have an obligation to those yet to be born, that they may live in a more Christlike world.

To the past, we owe our gratitude; to the present we owe our loyal service; to the future we dedicate our strength that it may, by thy grace, O God, be a better future. Amen.

A Community of Suffering

Week 40—Day 1   **Read Matt. 16:24; 20:22**

That medical missionary in the African jungle, Albert Schweitzer, whose service to people has won the admiration of millions, wrote this of his desire to help people, inspired by the love of God: "I could not but feel with a sympathy full of regret all the pain that I saw around me, not only that of men but that of the whole creation. From this community of suffering I have never tried to withdraw myself. It has seemed to me a matter of course, that we should all take our share of the burden of pain which lies upon the world."

May we not withhold ourselves from the community of suffering in the world, but take our share of the load. Amen.

Week 40—Day 2   **Read Luke 18:10-12**

A newspaper story from Cincinnati, Ohio, some years ago told that a man, sixty-one years old had broken a national record for remaining in a coma. He was in a coma for nine years! Yet there are people who seem to be in a coma for a longer time as far as any awareness of the condition of the world or of most anything except their own immediate comfort is concerned. A worker for a Community Chest stopped at a door and was greeted by a woman who said to him, "There ain't no use to stop here. We ain't interested in nothing." Probably true! The Pharisee in our scripture reference today never noticed the needs of others. He was in a "coma," all wrapped up in himself.

O God, our Father, awaken day by day our spirits to watchfulness. Amen.

Week 40—Day 3   **Read Prov. 17:17; Ps. 69:20**

A woman who has helped a great many people over tough spots in their lives said in an interview, "I have discovered that a great many people are lonely, more than you might suppose." Have you discovered that? Here is the way a young man, a stranger in a big city, described loneliness: "It grips you in the pit of the stomach, it crawls up your spine, and pokes right into your brain." It is not always that bad. But everyone ought to remember that a multitude of people, in the midst of crowds, are lonely. A hand of friendship is a real "lifesaver."

O thou who are the God of all comfort, help us to bring friendship and fortification to people. Amen.

Week 40—Day 4   **Read Luke 6:36-38**

We often hear, "He was a very reserved person." These words may be a tribute and often are. They may describe a person never loud, never aggressive or loquacious. But the words, on the other hand, may also be a reproach, a sort of a sad epitaph on a selfish life. For it often means that he reserved himself for his own interests. It often means, "He built a little picket fence around himself." People in need of friendship, of sympathy, of the outgoing of a generous heart, outsiders, and anyone in need get no farther than the fence! Are you a "reserved person"?

Help us, our Father, to be openhearted, to give of ourselves to others in full measure, pressed down and running over. Amen.

Week 40—Day 5   **Read Rom. 12:1, 11**

A few years ago Van Druten wrote a play about Berlin, Germany, when Hitler and the Nazis were coming to power. His play had a strange title *I Am a Camera*, which meant that the play merely recorded what the author saw as a camera might record it. He did not take sides or pass judgment. Ask yourself, am I more than a camera as I look out on the world, merely seeing its sin and suffering and need, or do I do something about those things?

As we lift up our eyes and see the world about us, O God, help us to lift up our hands also that we may take hold of the very many tasks that need to be done. Amen.

Week 40—Day 6   **Read John 4:6-10**

Have you ever thought about Jesus' use of time? He had a short life; he had much to do; yet he was in no breathless hurry. He seemed to have a different scale of values from most of us. There were many things which were vastly important to many people, but for them Jesus had no time. He had no time to amass property, for instance. But we see clearly that he did have time *for people*. He would give large amounts of time talking to people and helping them. He took a long time to talk to one woman at a wayside well. Again and again he made a detour in the midst of a busy day to go and heal people. To him the needs of people were the most important things in all of life.

Make us quick to see the needs of others and give us leisure from ourselves that we may put ourselves at the disposal of people to whom we may minister. Amen.

Week 40—Day 7   Read Prov. 6:10-11; Mark 13:35-36

We hear much about the evils of "isms," such as Communism and Fascism. We ought to remember that one of the evil "isms" in our world is somnambulism, that is, sleep walking. It is an evil thing for us to go about our world and neighborhood, walking in our sleep, seeming to be wide awake, but really not. We can be sound asleep to all the dangers that threaten the youth of our town, asleep to the needs of the church in ministering to the needs of all people, asleep to the needs of sustaining forces seeking to establish an enduring peace.

Wilt thou waken our spirits day by day. O God, that we may be alert to the dangers that threaten thy people near and far. For Jesus' sake. Amen.

WEEK 41

A Steady Succession of Days

Week 41—Day 1   **Read Acts 4:31-34**

George Cheeryholmes, a missionary in China when the Red regime took over, was arrested by an officer in the Communist army early one morning and taken before the local Commissar. This official, a typical small-minded functionary, hardly knew what to charge the missionary with. Finally he said to him, "I understand you are a Christian missionary. I don't know much about religion of any kind, but I suppose that if it is worth anything, it is worth dying for."

We would all agree that our religion is worth dying for. Here is a nearer, closer question, "Is it worth *living* for?" That is what we are called to do, to *live* for our faith, not in one dramatic act, but in a steady succession of days.

Our lives have come from thee, O God. Help us to live with a never diminished sense of responsibility and to live not to ourselves, but to thee. Amen.

Week 41—Day 2   **Read Acts 19:28-31**

Sholem Asch, the Jewish novelist who died a few months ago, writer of impressive novels about early Christianity, including *Mary* and *The Apostle*, went to Palestine in preparation for writing. He said, "I wanted to get the actual *feel* of the Holy Land." It would be wonderful, would it not, to get the *feel* of the early church? Well, we can do that. We can get the "feel" of the book of Acts by having the same experiences which the early Christians had—of seeking to win disciples, and standing up for our faith against crowd pressure.

O God, to us may grace be given to follow in the train of the early pioneers of our faith. Amen.

Week 41—Day 3　　　　　　　　**Read John 15:12-13**

　　　　　　　An American tourist traveling in Palestine was fond of telling of what he called "the miracle" at Nazareth. He was surrounded by the usual crowds of roadside merchants selling souvenirs. He felt that this yelling, pushing crowd everywhere was a terrible nuisance. But one woman surprised him. She said, "Buy something from the woman over there. She hasn't sold anything all day." Such love and sympathy was something new. He said, "Such unselfishness makes me believe in the love of Christ who grew up in Nazareth." Our unselfish acts do more to convince onlookers of the reality of the love of God than many words could do.

Help us to remember, O God, that it is by our acts that we bear witness to thy love. Amen.

Week 41—Day 4　　　　　　　　**Read Mark 10:42-45**

　　　　　　　In the will of Patrick Henry, the American patriot who made the celebrated speech before the Revolution beginning, "Give me liberty or give me death," there is an arresting paragraph:

"I have now disposed of all my property to my family. There is one thing more that I wish I could give to them. That is the Christian religion. If they had that, and I had not given them one shilling, they would have been rich; and if they had not that, and I had given them the world, they would be poor."

We cannot give away religious faith as we might give away a sum of money or a piece of jewelry. It can only be conveyed by example, and training, and contagion of spirit. To share what we have of religious faith is one of the highest privileges and duties we have.

Help us, O God, to share our best with as many people as we can reach. Amen.

Week 41—Day 5   **Read II Cor. 5:18-20**

Here is a bit of history which challenges us to bring our genuine devotion to our work and thought for the church. When Robert Louis Stevenson, the novelist, was dying in Samoa, he was anxious to finish the novel on which he was working. Due to the progress of disease he had lost his power to speak. So he learned the deaf-and-dumb language, and by that means dictated to his stepdaughter. What tremendous effort he gave that a novel might be finished! How much effort do we make, compared to that, so that something far better than any novel, the story of God's love, may reach people?

Quicken our hearts and minds, and strengthen our hands, O God, that we may be faithful messengers for thee. Amen.

It was high praise which Jesus gave to the woman who broke a jar of precious perfume to anoint him. He said, "She hath done what she could." It may not seem, at first glance, a great thing to praise. It may seem an ordinary thing to do what one can. But that is very often the very thing people will *not* do. They think of what they would do if things were different, if they had a million dollars, or a place of great power. But such reveries count for nothing. What does count is what you *can* do, not the million dollars we do not have, but the ten dollars we *do* have, the influence we can exert with what we have.

May we bring to thy service, O God, the offering of continual faithfulness, doing what we can. In Jesus' name. Amen.

John Wesley left strict directions that no biography of him be written. Yet such a man could not prevent a biography, telling of his services to mankind, from being written. No one of us can prevent our biography being written. It may not be written in a book or in articles printed in newspapers. *But it will be written in the lives of other people.*

Often, unconsciously, our actions are written down in the effect they have on other lives. Every kindness and every unkindness is being written.

May we so live that the memory of us will be a blessing to those lives we touched. Amen.

God Mend It All

Week 42—Day 1 **Read Eph. 6:10-15**

John Wycliffe, the first translator of the Bible into English, showed his heroic spirit in a dialogue later used as a motto for "Latter Day Pamphlets," by Thomas Carlyle. It is: "One man, looking at a great evil in the world said, 'Well, well, God mend it all.' 'No,' said the other, 'that is wrong. We must help him mend it.'" That is the spirit of the New Testament. We must help God mend the broken world we live in. It is not enough to sink back in limp lassitude and sigh, "God mend it." Are we doing anything to help God mend a single evil in the world?

Help us, O God, to be fellow workers with thee, and to prepare the way for thy coming in the life of the world. Amen.

Week 42—Day 2 **Read Col. 3:9-11**

The director of a boy's club made a very good answer to a question commonly asked. A very fussy woman, a good deal of a snob, was making inquiries about how the boy's club was run. "Is it true," she asked sternly, "that you allow colored boys in the same club with white boys?"

"Madam," the director answered, "in this club we do not deal in skins. We deal in boys."

Keep active and alive in our minds and hearts, O God, that thou art the Father of all people. In Christ's name. Amen.

A common expression, used by everyone, indicates a short distance, "within shooting distance." A person will say, "Our house is within shooting distance of the high school." But what a different meaning the words have from what they had only a few years ago. "Shooting distance" is now not a half mile or so, it is five thousand miles! Under the development of intercontinental missiles, Moscow is within "shooting distance" of Chicago. What our world needs now is for nations to be brought within "living distance." Men who are afar off must be brought together in obedience to Christ.

May the peace of Christ, O God, become the peace of the whole world. Amen.

A student of society has written that "the most representative man in our chaotic era is the 'other directed' person, the individual who develops sensitive antennae" to perceive what the majority is thinking and saying and hurries to agree with them.

At times, that seems all too true. What our nation and our world need are persons with sensitive antennae, all right—sensitive minds and spirits who can perceive the will of God and adjust themselves to doing that will no matter how great the majority around them oppose the truth of God revealed in Christ.

Help us, O God, to be about our Father's business in the world, and to keep our minds sensitive to the revelation of thy will, by prayer and the reading of thy word. In Jesus' name. Amen.

Week 42—Day 5   Read Luke 19:42; Isa. 2:4

A billboard advertisement in a large city bore these words, "Charter a bus and keep your party together." It is good advice for a picnic. It is good advice for a world of nations. The peace of the world depends on "keeping the party" of the various nations of the world together. That is our prayer for the United Nations that it may, in the Providence of God, become the agency for keeping nations together and establishing a world of law instead of a world of violence. To that end we should seek God's blessing and direction in the work of peace. As someone has said, "we will either be the best generation or the last."

Grant thy blessing and strength, O God, to all who are working to establish a linked and steadfast guard on peace. In the name of the Prince of Peace. Amen.

Week 42—Day 6   Read Matt. 25:1-13

Several years ago, an automobile driver in White Plains, New York, was indicted by a Westchester County grand jury on a charge of "culpable, criminal negligence" because he "fell asleep at the wheel." The jury was right. To go to sleep while driving a car is to endanger the lives of people. It is truly a criminal action. To go to sleep, in the sense of not paying attention to what is going on in our community and in the world, is a very evil thing. If there are forces making for evil in our community, or forces threatening the peace of the world, and we are sound asleep to the dangers, we are failing to be God's watchful servants. Jesus said, "Watch and pray."

Give us the diligent eye, that we may be alert to every opportunity to serve thee. Amen.

Week 42—Day 7   **Read Acts 17:24-26**

A profound thing on race relations was said a short time ago by the prime minister of Southern Rhodesia. He was speaking of the terrible race wars in Kenya which resulted in so much killing. The prime minister, looking to the future, said, "We will have to drop the color idea and regard him as just another man."

That is the true view of every man, whatever his race or color or nationality. He is just another man before the God who regards all men without discrimination.

Father of mankind, turn, we pray thee, the conflict among brothers into the blotting out, across every land, of all the hatreds and antagonisms which set men against each other. Amen.

Like Empty Cups

Week 43—Day 1   **Read Prov. 10:27-32**

One of the lovely things that has been said of the stories of the Bible was said a few years ago by Anne Morrow Lindbergh. She says of many of the stories, "They are so simple that they are like empty cups for people to fill with their own experience and drink for their own need over and over again, through the years." Think how the story of the lonely Jacob, who used a stone for a pillow, ministers to our own loneliness. The story of Joseph in Egypt, finding God's help in temptation, brings help to us. Think of the encouragement of Jesus' story of the widow's giving two pennies. Pass your cup to drink to your own need.

A glory gilds the sacred page, O Lord. May we not miss its shining light, which it throws on our path. In Jesus' name. Amen.

Week 43—Day 2   **Read I Cor. 13:4-7**

Meditate today on the phrase in the seventh verse of the wonderful thirteenth chapter of I Corinthians, "Love believes all things." That does not mean that love believes anything, no matter how foolish or impossible. Love is not gullible. The words really mean, "Love is always eager to believe the best." That is the way it is often translated. Are we eager to believe the best about people, often giving them support by our faith when appearances may be against them? Here is a way of love as the poet Yeats pictures it. "I have believed the best of every man and find that to believe the best is enough to make a bad man show him at his best, or even a good man swing his lantern higher."

Grant, O God, that we may be always hopeful, always patient, gladdened by goodness. Amen.

Week 43—Day 3   **Read Mark 9:33-35**

Henry D. Thoreau went out to live alone in a little hut on the shores of Walden Pond in Concord, Mass. This was the experiment in simple living which had such a far-reaching effect through the book, *Walden.*

Thoreau said of the venture, "It will be a success if I shall have left myself behind." We can say that about many things, can we not? Our life can be a success if we leave our insistent, demanding, voracious selves, always thinking of "me, me, me," behind, and think of other people and the world. Our religious faith will be a success if we can stop clamoring for things for ourselves and turn our minds to God.

Grant, O God, that thou wilt increase in our thoughts and actions and that our selfish concern may decrease. Amen.

Week 43—Day 4   **Read I Pt. 3:8-9**

We are often tempted to think that we cannot do anything to help in the misery and suffering of the world, or in preventing the mass destruction of war. But there *are* things we can do. If we cannot stop all reckless self-seeking, we can at least stop it in ourselves. If we cannot abolish cruel prejudice, we can at least abolish it out of our own mind and heart. We can be just and kind to people about us, regardless of race, creed and color, and in so doing help to create a spiritual climate favorable to peace.

O God, whom to know is health and peace and joy, make us the instruments of brotherhood and peace. Amen.

Week 43—Day 5   **Read Acts 20:35**

The ruins of Pompeii, in Italy, which was covered with ashes from the eruptions of Mount Vesuvius, began to be dug up in 1748. Before the digging had gone on very long, the workers found a skeleton stretched forth at full length, with gold and silver coins that had rolled out of bony hands, still seeking, it seemed, to clutch them fast. Strange, in the very act of death, still grasping the coins! But he "couldn't take them with him."

That is a fair picture of a tragic truth, that the endeavor to clutch coins has spoiled life for many people. For what shall it profit to clutch all the coins ever minted, if in the lust for gain, we lose our own life?

Give us, O God, the open hand of generous giving. Save us from hands clutching for greed. Amen.

Week 43—Day 6   **Read Matt. 6:22-24**

The recently published life of the great explorer, Henry M. Stanley, the man who found David Livingstone in the jungles of Africa, contains many little known facts of Stanley's early life. One remarkable fact of his early years in America is that he fought on both sides of the Civil War! Part of the time he fought in the Union Army, part of the time in the Confederate! Quite a trick!

But in religion, sometimes we fight on both sides. We sing, "Who is on the Lord's side?" The answer, we assume, is, "We are." But if we have unchristian attitudes, if we are spotty in our church attendance or stingy in our support, we are not on the Lord's side. If we have only lazy indifference to causes of brotherhood, justice, and peace, we are on the side of evil. Jesus demanded undivided allegiance.

Help us, O God, to give ourselves wholly to thy service. Amen.

Week 43—Day 7   **Read Acts 24:16**

Robert Haydon, the English artist, used his own face as a model for Christ on his massive painting of Christ entering Jerusalem. In other words, he made a Christ that looked very much like himself.

In other realms than painting we are tempted to do the same. We are tempted to think of Christ as very much like ourselves, consequently we are liable to think that what we like or what we do will be all right. If we take that "easy" kind of thinking, we will not face seriously the challenge which Christ's teaching makes to our compromises with evil, our laziness in unselfish action, our selfishness in pampering ourselves.

May we be honest and stern in all our self-judgments. Amen.

A Gorgeous Blue Mountain

Week 44—Day 1   **Read Ps. 121:1-8**

Someone wrote of his home in a Colorado town that there was a gorgeous blue mountain at the end of the street. It was always a thrill to look down the street, at dawn, or noon, or sunset. It is possible to say of a life of trust and faith that "God is at the end of our street." All of the daily happenings of life and the problems as well as the acts of life have the background of God's love. The eternal God makes the supreme background for daily life.

Into thy hands, O God, we commit each day, with all our works begun, continued and ended in thee. Amen.

Week 44—Day 2   **Read Jas. 4:13-15**

In one of James M. Barrie's short plays, a man rushes out into a London street, hails a cab, and says to the driver, "Drive back ten years!"

Ah, if we only could drive back ten years! How gladly we would do many things differently. But, "the moving finger writes, and having writ moves on, nor all your piety nor all your wit, shall lure it back to cancel half a line."

Remember two things: God can cancel the sins behind us by his forgiveness. Also, the remembrance that we cannot drive back increases the solemnity of each day's acts.

Help us to bring to each day's living the realization that we can live it only once, and help us to live it unto thee. For Jesus' sake. Amen.

Week 44—Day 3   **Read Isa. 40:29-31**

Think today of the line in the *Book of Common Prayer,* a line which serves well as a motto for today and for all the tomorrows. This prayer asks that all our works may be "begun, continued and ended in Thee." Our God is the God of new beginnings. We recognize that fact in prayer at the beginning of a new year or a new enterprise. Our God is also the God of the continuance of old enterprises. All our works may be continued in God's help, in the hard days, the dull days, the dark days as well as the bright ones.

Grant, O God, that each day's work may be begun, continued and ended in thee. Amen.

Week 44—Day 4   **Read John 13:2-5**

Charles Dickens in the 1840's said of Washington, D. C., that it had "spacious avenues that begin in nothing and lead nowhere." Those words, strangely enough, describe many lives. The life of a person without any religious faith seems to begin in nothing and lead to nothing, no sense of the meaning of life and no goal.

Contrast that with the description of Jesus, given in the story of the Last Supper, "Jesus, knowing that he came from God and went to God . . . girded himself." Christian faith gives

203

us a vision of the origin of life in God, and the destiny of life to God.

We thank thee, O God, for the revelation that our life came from thee and that we go to thee. Amen.

Week 44—Day 5 Read Ps. 34:4-8

A teacher talked much of his garden. His students wanted to see it. But when they got there, they were disappointed. "But, it is so small!" they said. "Yes," replied the teacher, pointing to the sky, "but look how high it is."

Our "garden," our situation may be small, but if our thoughts and prayers look up to the sky, it is a large place. If we reach up to God, we can say with the psalmist, "Thou hast set my feet in a large place."

Help us to remember that no place is a small place where thou art with us. We bring thee our thanks for the promise that thou wilt not leave us or forsake us. In Jesus' name. Amen.

Week 44—Day 6 Read I Tim. 6:11, 12

Vachel Lindsay wrote an arresting poem about Niagara Falls. He described men in Buffalo, important men in the city, who were busy buying and selling and rushing to and fro, and in all their years great Niagara was displaying its marvels a few miles away, and they had never seen it! So also, there were women in Buffalo, busy shopping for bargains, busy at card parties, who had never seen "great Niagara."

The poem pictures impressively people missing an amazing wonder which they might have experienced. It suggests the men and women who have missed the greatest experience possible on earth, a greater wonder than Niagara—the knowledge of God and the fellowship of God.

May we put first things first in our lives, O God, and not miss life's richest prize, that of knowing thee. Amen.

Week 44—Day 7   **Read John 15:15-16**

When John Masefield, Poet Laureate of Great Britain, was a young man, he left the sea and went to work in a carpet mill in Yonkers, N. Y. Of that change he said later, "Compared to the life at sea, the life in the mill lacks the companionship of the sky." What a beautiful phrase! And how picturesquely it describes what Christian faith brings to us, "the companionship of the sky." We have the companionship of heaven, of the God who is our father, and of Christ, our elder brother! That high companionship is expressed in the words of Jesus to his disciples, "I have called you friends."

We are grateful, O God, that thou hast given us the gift of friendship with thee. Help us to be worthy of that high relationship. In Jesus' name. Amen.

A Knock at the Door

Week 45—Day 1   **Read Rev. 3:20-22**

Think for a few moments today of the word of Jesus as recorded in Revelation: "Behold I stand at the door and knock." Now, in your imagination, add to that verse this sentence written by Charles Lamb: "Not many sounds in life, and I include all urban and rural sounds, exceed in interest a knock at the door."

That is true, isn't it? How much more interesting than any other is the knock pictured in our scripture: "Behold I stand at the door and knock!" Open the door and let Christ into your desires and plans.

May we make room in our hearts, O God, for all the remembrances that will help us to be our best. Amen.

Week 45—Day 2   **Read I Cor. 2:9-12**

We all know the thrilling story of Robinson Crusoe. The original of that story, the man who really was cast on a desert island, was Alexander Selkirk. He is well remembered by the poem beginning, "I am monarch of all I survey. My right there is none to dispute." He was rescued after being on the island alone for four years. The sailors from the rescuing ship found him on the beach wildly waving his arms to them. They reported, "He was a Scotchman, but he had so much forgotten his language for want of use that we could scarce understand him." Let those words sink into your mind, "He had forgotten his language for want of use." We can forget the great language of our faith, such thrilling words as "Our Father," "forgive us our trespasses," "Thy Kingdom come." We should use that language every day if we are not to forget it.

Thou hast put great words on our lips, O God. We thank thee for the language of our Father's house. Help us to keep that language in our hearts and on our lips. Amen.

Week 45—Day 3   **Read Matt. 6:22-24**

At a Methodist conference a few years ago the event of greatest general interest was the election of new bishops. On the last Sunday of the conference the new bishops were consecrated to their office. A little girl of eight, the daughter of a delegate, told her friends that she was "going down to see the new bishop 'concentrated.'" Quite an idea—for a person to be concentrated! But the right idea—to concentrate all our powers and energies on what we are doing. Paul was "concentrated" when he said, "This one thing I do." We are "concentrated" when we do not scatter our loyalty but give allegiance to one master—Christ.

Grant, O God, our Father, that we may have one commanding loyalty to thee. Amen.

Week 45—Day 4   **Read Ps. 15**

In his early years in the musical world Frank Sinatra had himself incorporated and some other men "owned" a part of him. That is, they had put out money for his expenses and were entitled to a share of the profits from his singing. Sinatra finally "bought himself" from those who "owned" part of him, and so he finally "owned" himself! How about us? In a figurative sense do we own ourselves, or do others determine what we shall think, what we shall do, whom we shall follow? Can we say, with determination, "I know not what course others may take, but as for me and my house, we will serve the Lord"? That is really owning yourself!

Grant, O God, that we may not be conformed to this world, but set ourselves firmly to obey thee. Amen.

Week 45—Day 5   Read Matt. 13:54-58

Note the words, "And he did not many works there because of their unbelief." We can hinder God's work in our midst because of our unbelief. The atomic scientist, Dr. Leo Szillard, said of the future, so dark with the threat of atomic destruction, "Maybe God will work a miracle if we do not make it too hard for Him." Our world needs the miracle of God's grace and love. May we offer no obstruction to God's work by the unbelief of our hearts, but may we make possible the words, "Thy faith hath made thee whole."

Pour out thy spirit, we beseech thee, O Lord, upon us and upon the church, that we may have new visions, new life and new obedience to Christ. Amen.

Among the saddest words in the gospels are these from the sixth chapter of John, "Many of his disciples went back, and walked no more with him." They had the high prize of fellowship with Christ, and they gave it up. They "walked no more." Why was it? Probably there were many reasons. Some, no doubt, saw that it would be dangerous to walk farther with Jesus. In others, perhaps, enthusiasm died down. Some expected the wrong things. Are those not the very things that keep disciples of Jesus today from following him, fear of difficulty, the cooling down of devotion, wanting the wrong things from Christ?

To us, O God, has been given the high prize of life, that of walking with Jesus as his disciples. May nothing separate us from obedience to Christ. Amen.

Our scripture reference for today declares that we have entered into the blessed results of other men's labors. Consider this true picture of that truth: "When a medical missionary enters a community, he is accompanied by a thousand men, among whom are Pasteur with his knowledge of bacteriology, Fleming with his discovery of penicillin, Jefferson with his understanding of the democratic way of life, Jerome and Tyndale with their translations of the Bible, and Paul with his interpretations of Christianity."

There are two things we should do in regard to these gifts of others. The first is to receive gratefully the gifts which we have not earned. The second thing is to do our work so thoroughly and devotedly that others may enter into our labors.

On every hand, O God, we are surrounded by gifts which come to us through others. Increase our humility and thankfulness to thee and to others. Having received fully, may we give fully. Amen.

What a Good Boy Am I

Week 46—Day 1   **Read Luke 18:9-13**

We all remember the comic history of Little Jack Horner. "He stuck in his thumb and pulled out a plum, and said, 'What a good boy am I.'" A grown up Little Jack Horner is a sad spectacle. We can stand a child covering himself with praise. We smile and call him "cute." But when a grown person purrs with self-satisfaction, like a cat which is well pleased with himself, the sight and sound are disgusting. We know from Jesus' parable of the Pharisee and the Publican that God does not value self-satisfaction. The Pharisee was not "justified." That is, he was not acceptable. Do not say, "What a good boy am I," but say, "God, be merciful to me, a sinner."

Give us, O God, the grace of humiliy that we may truly be followers of Jesus. In his name. Amen.

Week 46—Day 2   **Read Luke 6:41-42**

A boy in grammar school was writing an examination in the physiology class. To the question, "What are the principal parts of the eye?" he answered, "The principal parts of the eye are the mote and the beam." At least he gave evidence he had been to Sunday school and knew the Bible, and, in an important way, he was right. There are important parts of the eye, such as the cornea and retina, that he did not

211

mention. But how important the mote and the beam are in our life! How important it is to see our own evils more clearly than we see the lesser evils of others.

Help us to see ourselves as thou dost see us, O God, and to seek thy power to correct our faults. Amen.

Week 46—Day 3   Read Luke 12:33-34

Rudyard Kipling gave a commencement address some years ago at McGill University, Montreal, Canada. After advising the graduates against an over-concern for wealth, position, or glory, he said, "Some day you will meet a man who cares for none of these things . . . and then you will know how poor you are!"

What an unintended description of Jesus! He cared for none of these things, and when we look steadily at him, he makes us think how poor we are. Think on this quality of Jesus.

Forbid it, O God, that we may amass only the riches of the world, in large or small measure, and fail to be rich toward God. In Jesus' name. Amen.

Week 46—Day 4   Read Luke 18:10-14

The Scotch preacher and novelist, George McDonald, once said something which sounds strange, but when we think it over carefully, we will see that it has wisdom. He wrote, "I need God's help not only when I am doing evil, but when I am doing good. For it is then that the sin of self-righteousness and pride and conceit may tempt me. Am I going to do a good deed? Then of all times—Father, into Thy hands, lest the enemy should have me now." We need to pray for God's grace that we may never lose true humility and that we may forget ourselves in devotion to God and his kingdom.

May all feeling of our own goodness drop from us and may we say with sincerity, God, be merciful to me, a sinner. Amen.

Week 46—Day 5   **Read Luke 6:41-43**

Near the entrance to an art gallery in London, there used to be a wastebasket. A visitor once asked the guard at the entrance what the basket was for. He answered with a smile, "That is where the students drop their conceit when they go out." He had noticed over the years many students enter the gallery and then see some really great paintings, and the sight of such truly fine work took away their conceit over their own work. So the sight of Jesus takes away our self-satisfaction over our imagined excellences, and only one prayer rises to our lips, "God, be merciful to me, a sinner."

Help us, O God, to see the vision of Christ so clearly, that we may see our failings in the light of his goodness and be moved to repentance. Amen.

Week 46—Day 6   **Read Prov. 7:1-4**

A well-known poem of eight lines, declares impressively that there are two ghosts that haunt every one of us. One is the "child we used to be." The other is the "man we might have been." We often feel that we have not fulfilled all the hopes that the child had for himself. We often feel that we have missed being "the person we might have been." Such thoughts are good for us if they keep us humble and if they cause us to struggle to overtake our finest possibilities.

We are grateful, O God, that life is not over for us. Help us to put into all our remaining days and years all our strength into making ourselves what thou dost desire us to be. Amen.

Week 46—Day 7   **Read Luke 22:25-27**

One question which demands an answer from us is a strange one, "How do you talk to yourself?" There is no use in saying, "I do not talk to myself." We all do. Not audibly, perhaps, but in the inward debates we all have. Do you say to yourself, "You poor thing. You're having a hard time. I'm sorry for you. Life isn't fair to you." That kind of talk breaks down strong character. Our talk to ourselves should be like this: "Do your best always. For even your best is not worthy of your Master!"

Save us, O God, from self-pity. Help us to set high standards for ourselves, that we may be good servants of our Master. In his name. Amen.

WEEK 47

On Top of His Material

Week 47—Day 1   **Read I Cor. 9:24-27**

A magazine writer paying tribute to a writer of short stories said as the climax of an article of appreciation: "This man is constantly on top of his material." His material did not get the best of him.

A fine tribute in life to say that a person "is on top of his material." For very often one's material is on top of him. The material of wealth and possessions, of busy affairs, and the material of dissipation, gets on top of the soul and crushes it.

Help us, O God, to seek first the kingdom of God and his righteousness. Amen.

Week 47—Day 2   **Read Matt. 6:16-18**

Here is a personal question. Does our usual expression give the impression that Christian faith brings joy? It ought to do that. Toscanini, the orchestra leader, said sharply to a soloist who was rehearsing for a rendering of Beethoven's *Ninth Symphony*, "Do you know what you are singing about? You are singing of brotherhood, but in your face you look as if you hate everyone. Let the meaning of the words show in your face!"

Grant, O God, that we may go forth into each day with gladness. Amen.

215

We often hear the phrase "extended himself." It often describes an exceptionally fine performance, such as an athletic event, or making a speech, for instance. Sometimes the words suggest other meanings. A man may "extend himself" like an octopus, reaching out his tentacles to snatch some advantages from someone else. Strongly acquisitive people remind us of a long claw reaching out to snatch.

There is a better way of "extending yourself." It is the extension of the perceiving, experiencing, and sharing self. Jesus wanted people to extend themselves into other lives, beyond the walls of their own comfort and gain.

Help us, O God, to remember the plea of Jesus that we be concerned for others as well as ourselves. Amen.

A delegate to a large national church convention kept raising objections all the time to proposals to action. Finally, a friend said to him in irritation, "For goodness sake, Fred, get on the positive side of *something*, even if it is only to move to open the windows."

The friend had a good point. If we are always on the negative side, criticizing, objecting, pouring cold water over everything, we soon get to be not only tiresome bores, but also obstructions to good causes.

Help us, O God, to retain positive enthusiasms for all good undertakings. Amen.

A high-school student asked a very penetrating question about Roman history: "There were lots of religions in Rome in the first two centuries of the Christian era: how come the Christians were the only ones persecuted?" A good question. There is a good answer. The Christians were the only ones persecuted, because they were the only ones whose religion was a real threat to the ways of life about them. As was said truly about them, "these that have turned the world upside down hath come hither also" (Acts 17:6). They were dangerous to the paganism of the empire and to its cruelty, its lust, its emperor worship. Are we dangerous to evil or harmless?

Help us to be worthy of being opposed by evil forces, O God. Amen.

Some people seem to have made their aim in life to avoid the disagreeable. They keep well out of sight of human need, or suffering, or wrong. Such a man was once prime minister of Great Britain, Lord Melbourne. He closed his eyes, as far as he could, to all unpleasant things. He never even read anything that dealt with the grim and sordid, such as Dickens' story of *Oliver Twist*. Remember how Jesus praised the good Samaritan who took care to see and to help the man lying wounded on the road? In fact Jesus lived most of his active years looking at suffering and need. Do you turn away from the disagreeable and ugly in our world and thus make yourself useless in bringing any help?

Save us, O God, from all selfish and cowardly blindness to the need about us. Amen.

Week 47—Day 7

Read Heb. 12:1-2

Will you meditate, and for more than a moment, on the words of our scripture for today, "the sin that doth so easily beset us?" What *are* the sins that so easily beset us? We cannot take credit for resisting sins that have no real attraction for us. Many persons abstain from alcoholic liquor, not so much because they have strong wills as because they have weak stomachs. They do not like the stuff, so it is no trouble at all to resist it! Most people deserve no credit for abstaining from robbery or arson. But, then, what *are* the sins that beset *us?* That is, the sins which beset some rather prosperous, middle class citizens of fine integrity? How about complacency, the sin of self-satisfaction, self-righteousness, partisanship, race discrimination, indifference?

Help us, our Father, to lay aside every weight and the sins that do so easily beset us, and to run with patience the race that is set before us, looking unto Jesus. Amen.

A Constant Pageant of Triumph

Week 48—Day 1   **Read Ps. 91:14-16**

Drop these lines of Emily Dickinson into your imagination. They move to a lively beat. Look particularly at the line, "He danced along the dingy ways." Most of us know too much about "dingy ways"! Often we think that our address might be correctly given as "No. 101 Dingy Way." But a true faith in God does give wings with which to move along any dingy way. Paul proved it. He had all kinds of troubles, yet he said, "Christ makes my life a constant pageant of triumph."

O thou who art the Sun of Righteousness, drive away all darkness from our hearts. May we go through all our days upheld by trust in thee and with the joy of the Lord in our hearts. Amen.

Week 48—Day 2   **Read I Cor. 2:14-16**

If someone were to say to us, "I hope you lose your mind," we would think either that he had lost his own mind or else were full of hatred to us. But there is a true sense in which it is life's highest blessing to lose our mind. It follows from the verse in I Cor. 2:16, "We have the mind of Christ." That means we have "lost our minds" in his larger, higher mind. We have lost our stubborn, self-seeking, pushing mind,

and taken his mind as our guide and transformer. To lose our
own insistent mind and to bring every thought into captivity to
the obedience of Christ is our highest privilege.

*Make me a captive, Lord, and then I shall be free. Enable us
increasingly to be Christ's men and women. Amen.*

Week 48—Day 3   **Read Ps. 84:9-12**

On the cover of a periodical with a large
circulation some months ago, was a picture of the awesome
fireball of the hydrogen bomb, the greatest power that man has
ever controlled. If that were the final story of life and death,
this would be indeed an age of despair, but that is not the final
story as even that magazine bears witness. On a later page is a
picture of the risen Lord, and underneath these words, "Then
sang the sons of Eden . . . Glory, glory, glory to the Holy
Lamb of God." The greatest power in the universe is not the
fireball, but God as he comes to us in Christ.

May we hear always the words, "Hope thou in God." Amen.

Week 48—Day 4   **Read Jas. 1:2-5**

There is an amusing and fantastic episode
in a novel about Don Camillo, a character who has charmed
a large number of readers. Camillo is an Italian priest who has
many trials and conflicts with some people in his village. His
patience often wears thin. One day he utters a sigh, while in the
empty church. "Lord," he asks, "who can understand these people?" To his great surprise, a statue of the crucified Christ an-

220

swers, "I can." That is only a fantasy, of course. But it does point to a truth, that Christ does know and understand us. Also, we should try, instead of exploding at people and losing patience to understand them and to show love to them.

The Lord direct our hearts into the patience of Christ. Amen.

Week 48—Day 5   **Read John 8:12**

T. R. Glover, a great Christian scholar, once said a thing about poetry which suggests one high service which Jesus renders to us. Glover said, "If we are to get anything from a poet, we have not only to criticize him by ourselves, an easy and not always profitable task, but to criticize ourselves by him." That is what the person of Jesus Christ does for us, or may do for us if we allow him. We criticize ourselves by him. He said, "Follow me." We look at his courage, his unfailing love, his patience, his sacrifice, and we criticize ourselves by him.

O God our Father, whose glory has shined in the face of Jesus Christ, stir us with the desire to make our lives more like his. For his sake. Amen.

Week 48—Day 6   **Read Gal. 2:20; 6:14**

A pastor was trying to persuade a woman to teach a class in the church school. She was well-qualified and had time for it. She declined, saying over and over, "I don't want to be tied down to things." Finally, the pastor had all of that he could take. He looked her in the eye and said in a kindly voice, "You know we serve a Master who was willing to be *nailed* down to things. He was nailed to a cross."

Keep alive in our minds and heart the memory of Calvary where the dear Lord was crucified, who died to save us all. Freely we have received of his sacrifice. Freely may we give of our service. Amen.

Week 48—Day 7   **Read Acts 4:8-11**

The German phrase, *Wie befinden Siesich?* which is the equivalent of the English "How are you?" means, literally "How do you find yourself?" It is an attractive phrase as a greeting. But look at it literally and with imagination. Ask, "How *do* you find yourself?" That is, how does a person find his best possibilities, his genuine capacities?

We find ourselves, for one thing, in commitment to Christ. That was how Peter really found his best self. When he became a disciple, he unlocked new possibilities. We also "find ourselves" in service to causes that are greater than ourselves. Jesus said to some fishermen, "Follow me and I will make you fishers of men." When those fishermen gave themselves to the service of Jesus, they found larger selves within themselves. As it was in the beginning, it is now.

Savior, may we hear thy call, Give our lives to thine obedience, Serve and love thee best of all. Amen.

I Shall Win Either Way

Week 49—Day 1   **Read II Tim. 4:6-8**

In his last illness a friend visited George Tomlinson, a great Christian, once Minister for Education in England. The friend asked Thomlinson where he found comfort in his last days. He replied, "I find comfort in this, that I shall win either way. If I get better, I shall go to Blackpool and rest with my wife. If I don't get better I shall go to heaven and rest with my Saviour."

A true word. With faith in God we win either way, either here on earth, or in the eternal world. We can't lose.

Our times are in thy hands, O God. Deepen our fellowship with thee here on earth and our faith in eternal life with thee. Amen.

Week 49—Day 2   **Read   Rev. 3:20-21**

In a book about nature occur these words about spring, "To snatch the passing moment and examine it for signs of eternity is the noblest of occupations." That makes a great theme for today's meditations. There are signs of eternity in passing moments. When we read the Bible, not hurriedly, but thoughtfully, the passing moment brings us signs of God's will and his desires for us. The passing moment will

223

bring us opportunity to serve God and that brings eternity in our daily life.

We thank thee, O God, that thou art ever seeking to come into our lives. May we open the door to thy entrance. In the spirit of Jesus. Amen.

Week 49—Day 3   Read Mark 12:28-31

It was said of the grandfather of Emily Dickinson that "he believed like fury." "Fury" seems a strange word to use of belief. But, after all, isn't the word fitting? Jesus said, "Thou shalt love the Lord thy God with all thy heart, and with all thy soul, and with all thy mind, and with all thy strength." That sounds like a "furious" belief in God, does it not? It is belief with all that one has and is. Our faith in God should not be held languidly, or casually, or lazily, as though it does not make much difference. It makes a world of difference, and we should "believe like fury."

Help us, O God, that we may give our faith to thee without reservation, and that whatever our hands find to do for thee and with thee, we may do it with all our might. Amen.

Week 49—Day 4   Read Rom. 8:37-39

What a vital faith in a loving God can mean in life is seen by a picture of the lack of it, found in a novel about classical Rome entitled *Marius the Epicurean*. Marius concluded that "the maximum a well-ordered life could win from events was a candid discontent." That is a pretty slim

224

purse for a long journey! We can all manage to have a "candid discontent." But a genuine faith in a God of love brings infinitely more into life than discontent. It enables us to say, in any condition, "I am persuaded that neither death nor life . . . nor any other creature, shall be able to separate me from the love of God."

Lift us, we pray, O God, out of discontent with our lot, into faith that we can be more than conquerors in thy strength. Amen.

Week 49—Day 5   **Read Luke 13:1-5**

We are all familiar with the prayer of the disciple of Jesus, "Lord, increase our faith." In the midst of discouragements we must all pray that prayer. But we should make also another prayer, the very opposite of that: "Lord, increase our doubt." We are exposed on every hand to statements that are *not true.* When we are told that there is nothing the matter with the world that more science cannot cure, let us pray, "Lord, increase our doubt!" When we are told, as so many people seem to believe, that wealth is the highest prize of life, may we pray, "Lord increase our doubt."

Help us, O God, to see that the things that matter most in life are the things that matter most to Jesus. Amen.

Week 49—Day 6   **Read Ps. 27:11-14**

A word worth remembering was spoken by Ralph Waldo Emerson. A man rushed up to him one day and

225

announced feverishly that the world was "going to end tomorrow."

"Very well," replied Mr. Emerson calmly, "I can get along without it." That was a quaint expression of faith in God, but it is true. That is a faith to sustain us to the very end of life. We *can* get along without the world, for underneath are the everlasting arms.

Enlarge our minds and hearts, O God, that we may freely trust thy word that thou wilt not leave nor forsake us. Amen.

Week 49—Day 7   **Read Ps. 97:1-6**

Many have noticed that the Psalms used in the service of the Episcopal Church are from an earlier translation than the King James Version of 1611. Many of the translations are arresting. Consider the fourth verse of the 97th Psalm. In the King James Version we read, "His lightnings enlightened the world." The earlier translation of the verse reads, "His lightnings put a shine on the world." The meaning is the same, but the words "put a shine on the world" bring pictures to the imagination. Sometimes the world loses its "shine." It becomes dull and dark. Faith in God and in his love and care does bring a "shine" to existence. It is a bright world if the Light of the world is allowed to come into our thinking and trust.

Send forth thy light and truth, O God, and in thy light, may we see light. Amen.

Ask Largely

Week 50—day 1   **Read Luke 11:5-9**

Consider Jesus' parable of the friend at midnight. A householder had to provide food for an unexpected guest. He went to a friend and asked for three loaves. He asked for a great deal so that he would have enough for his guest and not "run short."

This parable has much to teach about prayer. It says to us, "Ask largely," so that you may give strength to others. The danger many people run into is to get just enough religious experience to "get by" on. They run their lives on a minimum of prayer, of service, of belief. Don't live on a minimum. "Friend, lend me three loaves."

Thou art more ready to give, O Lord, than we are to receive. May we open our hearts and lives to thy gifts that we may share with others. Amen.

Week 50—Day 2   **Read Dan. 6:10**

In these days when diplomacy is heavily relied on by nations to come to agreements, we hear much of "top-level conferences." That is, conferences taken part in, not only by ambassadors and foreign ministers, but by the heads of states. It is a conference at the highest level of power. In a very real sense prayer is something like that. It is a "top-level conference" in which we bring our problems, our desires, our intentions, our confessions to God. We look at everything in the light of his words, of his wisdom and love. He has promised, "I will guide them with my eye."

Help us to bring ourselves before thee that we may walk in the light as Christ is in the light. Amen.

Week 50—Day 3   **Read Dan. 6:10**

In H. G. Wells' novel *Ann Veronica* the heroine cries out at a crisis in her life when things had piled up in overwhelming amount, "O God, how I wish I had been taught to pray!"

There is a great lack in resources for facing life when one has not been taught to pray. *You* have been taught to pray. Do thank God for the loving souls who taught you. But we must all remember that if we do not keep up the practice of prayer, all the lessons we have had will soon drop from us. And prayer will become a forgotten power. Paul said, "Pray without ceasing."

For those servants of thine, parents, friends, teachers, who guided our steps in the way of Christ, we give thee our thanksgiving. Help us to keep all we have learned as a possession. In Jesus' name. Amen.

Week 50—Day 4   **Read Luke 11:9-13**

Everyone asks at times, just what happens when we pray? Sometimes the question on dark days is, does anything happen? Here is one answer by the famous physician and research genius in medicine, Alexis Carrel:

"The results of prayer can be measured in terms of increased physical buoyancy, greater intellectual vigor, moral stamina, and deeper understanding of the realities underlying physical relationship. How does prayer fortify us with such dynamic power? When we pray we link ourselves with the inexhaustible power that spins the universe. We ask that a part of this power be apportioned to our needs. Even in asking, our human deficiencies are filled, and we arise strengthened and repaired."

May we live a life of prayer, of thanksgiving, of petition for our needs, of intercession for others. In Jesus' name. Amen.

Week 50—Day 5   **Read Luke 11:1-4**

Some people have found help in the practice of prayer by objects that give concreteness of petition. One minister keeps three pictures on the wall in his study: a photograph of the church of which he is the minister, a panoramic view of the city in which he lives and works, and a reproduction of Holman Hunt's painting, "The Light of the World." Again and again he prays, bringing Christ in relation to the church and the city. Another man keeps a globe in the corner of a room and often turns it around and makes intercession for the peoples in the different parts of the world as they pass before his imagination. Others have made use of a morning newspaper, which often brings to mind people who stand in very great need.

May we always remember that thou art closer to us than

*breathing, and nearer than hands or feet. Help us to renew
thy life within us by prayer. Amen.*

Week 50—Day 6   **Read Matt. 6:28-33**

                In the museum of Natural History in New
York, a father was explaining the evolution of the horse's hoof
to his young son. The little boy grew restless, and tugged at his
father's sleeve and said, "Daddy, turn off your mind. Let's go
see the whale!"

We smile at that. But in a deeper sense, what we need greatly
at times is to "turn off our minds." We need to turn off the
restless anxieties and fears and worries. That we can do in the
prayer of trust.

*Grant, O God, that we may cast all our care upon thee, know-
ing that thou carest for us. In Jesus' name. Amen.*

Week 50—Day 7   **Read Matt. 6:6-8**

                Do we pray only when we *want* something
from God? What would you think of a man who rarely speaks
to his neighbor except when he wants to borrow from him?
Prayer descends to that level with some people. There is a truer
aspect of prayer, than that of him who said, "After this manner
pray ye, our Father . . . hallowed be Thy name."

This is a prayer at the Christian level: "Now, Father, in thy
dear presence kneeling, our spirits yearn to feel thy kindling
love; now make us strong; we need thy deep revealing of trust
and strength and calmness from above."

We need thee every hour, O God. Teach us thy will. Amen.
230

WEEK 51

Dead Money

The words "dead money" are used by bankers in a technical sense to mean money which has been deposited in banks but whose owners are never heard from. Three years ago there was in national banks more than $50,000,000 in 2,329,678 accounts. No trace could be found of the owners. Quite a lot of lost money!

In another sense consider the words "dead money." Money that does not contribute to the betterment of life is dead money. Money that goes into mere selfish display, into dissipation that breaks down both body and character, money merely hoarded, like gold in the clutch of a miser, is "dead money."

Help us to make our spending a true ministry to human welfare. Amen.

If you were asked the question, "What was the world's largest financial transaction," how would you answer it? The chances are that most of us would think of the merging of enormous companies, such as the formation of the United States Steel Company, or we would think of the sale of billions of dollars worth of U. S. Bonds. Wrong! The largest financial transaction in history took place when a poor widow in Jerusalem dropped two small coins—all her living—into an alms box. Jesus saw her and praised her sacrificial deed. Her action has inspired more giving, more money changing hands, than any other event in nineteen centuries. Sacrificial giving is big business.

O God, who art the Great Giver, deepen within us the conviction that it is more blessed to give than to receive. Open our hearts that we may give of our money, cheerfully and not of necessity. Amen.

Week 51—Day 3   **Read Matt. 10:7-9**

Often it is true that it is a poor rule that does not work both ways. Here is a good rule—"Freely ye have received. Freely give." Turn it around and it is also true. We can say truly—"Freely ye have given, freely receive." When we freely give to others of our time, of our strength, of our money, we receive fully of the deep joy of giving, of being a part of the force in the world working for a more abundant life for others.

May we cast our bread upon the waters, with generous sharing. Amen.

Week 51—Day 4   **Read II Cor. 9:6-8**

In II Cor. 9:7 we read of the three kinds of giving, "grudgingly," "of necessity," and "cheerfully." They are really the three degrees of giving, the lowest "grudgingly," somewhat higher "of necessity," and the highest, the giving that God loves, "cheerful" giving.

232

This applies to the giving of money, of time, of strength. We can make our gifts "grudgingly." That spoils the gift. We can do it because we have to. We do our duty, but there is no joy in it. Or we can give "cheerfully," remembering how freely we have received of God's love in Christ. What degree of giving is ours?

May we know the true joy of the Lord in giving, not because we have to, but because we love thee, O God. Amen.

Week 51—Day 5   **Read Matt. 25:24-28**

An elderly man once brought to Rossetti, the poet and painter, some sketches he had made. Rossetti looked at them sorrowfully and said the drawings were worthless. Then the old man laid before him some sketches done by a student. Rossetti was enthusiastic and said the student should be encouraged. The old man was moved to tears. He said, "I was that student!' He had had power, but he had allowed it to be wasted. There are many kinds of power. We are all stewards of God's gifts to us. We *must* save them from being wasted.

We thank thee, O God, for all the many gift which thou hast lent to us. May we dedicate all our powers to the highest use. In Jesus' name. Amen.

Week 51—Day 6   **Read I Cor. 4:1-5**

There is a real sadness in one of the last remarks of F. Scott Fitzgerald, the novelist who pictured life as it was to many people in the "jazz age" of the 1920's. He said,

"I have been only a mediocre steward of my talent." All too true! He had great talent as a novelist, but he died an early death with much of his promise unfulfilled, partly due to dissipation. In those words, there is a real recognition of the obligation of stewardship. He said at the same time, "I had a feeling that I was standing at twilight on a deserted range, with an empty rifle in my hand, and the targets down." These words ought not to be joined together, "mediocre" and "stewardship." In the New Testament we read something infinitely better, "It is required of stewards that a man be found faithful" (I Cor. 4:2).

O God, from whom has come to us all that we have, grant that we may be faithful stewards. Amen.

Week 51—Day 7   Read Luke 17:15-16

Something to remember every day is our obligation to others, most of whom we do not know, have not seen, and usually do not give a thought to. One of the greatest scientists of our time, Albert Einstein, put this truth vividly in his words, "A hundred times a day I remind myself that my inner and outer life depend on the labors of other men, living and dead, and that I must exert myself in order to give in the same measure as I have received and am receiving."

Help us, O God, to think of all the rich gifts that come to us from others. May we receive thankfully and give gladly of our strength. Amen.

WEEK 52

Open Outward

Week 52—Day 1   **Read Matt. 28:18-20**

In the state of Connecticut there is a law which requires that all church doors should open outward. Many churches have spent considerable sums of money making changes in their doors to conform to that law. It is a good law for church buildings and will prevent disasters in case of fire. But it is also a good law for the church as an organization and fellowship. All its thought and work and life should open outward, doors open to the world of need. There should be in all the life of the church the echo of the words of the Lord of the church, "Go ye into all the world." The same thing is true of one life. It should open outward to other people, to other groups, to other lands. For we are disciples of an outgoing Christ.

O thou, who didst come to bring deliverance to the captives, bring us out of the prison houses of our own selfish interests. Amen.

Week 52—Day 2   **Read Prov. 17:17**

Today let us meditate on elbows. In England in recent years, there has been a heavy penalty against "the misuse of elbows." This penalty probably has been the result of the war, when there have been so many people stand-

235

ing in line to buy food and to get tickets for movies and other affairs. It was a misdemeanor to push or gouge with the elbow. Quite right!

But there is a very good use of the elbow. That is to let another person feel the presence of an elbow at his side. The elbow of friendship and companionship in sorrow can be the most eloquent thing in the world. How do we use our elbows?

Teach us, O God, the high uses of friendship and sympathy like that of Jesus, in whose name we pray. Amen.

Week 52—Day 3   **Read Eph. 4:1-6**

If Christianity is to win against the forces of evil, it will not be done by people fighting singly and by themselves. As one pastor has illustrated this need for working together in churches, "Light is up against darkness: do you think your little single candle is enough to rout it? One light or two or a hundred will not do it, but the lights of a whole city will light a night sky, and you can see the glow for miles."

In these days we need to stand together, all believers in God, all people in all churches side-by-side. In the spirit of our Master, Jesus Christ. Amen.

Week 52—Day 4   **Read Ps. 103:1-5**

When Arnold Bennett, the British novelist, finished correcting proofs of a novel, he wrote in his diary, "I notice the far too frequent use of the word 'extraordinary,' but I am loath to alter a word once it is written."

In the life of the Christian there can never be too frequent use of the word "extraordinary." All of God's mercies are extraordinary, beyond all we can ask or think. Life itself, the wonderful pageant of nature, the immeasurable gift of friends, these are extraordinary. Never allow them to be regarded as ordinary!

We bring, O God, all that is within us to praise thee for thy continuing blessings. Amen.

Week 52—Day 5   Read I John 1:1-3

The German writer, Goethe, said a great word which comes close to the religious life of each one of us. "That which thy fathers have bequeathed to thee, earn it anew if thou wouldst possess it." God cannot give to us his best gifts unless in a real way we are willing to earn them for ourselves. God cannot give to us, as a package might be delivered, a strong religious faith. We must earn that by our own experience. We cannot have presented to us, as if on a silver platter, the joy of being fellow workers with God. We must win that joy by actually working.

Teach me Thy patience; still with Thee
In closer, dearer company,
In work that keeps faith sweet and strong,
In trust that triumphs over wrong.

Week 52—Day 6   Read Acts 1:7-8

Jesus makes clear that the gospel is to be carried to the ends of the earth. The words, "the uttermost part"

237

leaves no doubt about that. A Christian profession which feels that the non-Christian peoples should not be disturbed is a very inadequate sort of Christianity. A noble Christian leader of a generation ago, William F. McDowell, has met this false-hood with devastating force. He has put into a single sentence the heart of the Christian gospel. In reply to those who say that non-Christian peoples are "getting along pretty well without Christ," he said many times with burning emotion: *"No one is getting along pretty well without Jesus Christ."*

We make our prayer, O God, for the younger churches in overseas lands. Give them strength for difficult days. Help us to follow our prayers with our acts. Amen.

Week 52—Day 7   Read Matt. 28:19-20

The American poet, James Russell Lowell, wrote of "men with empires in their brains." Let us take that for our meditation today, as a true description of men and women devoted to foreign missions and the world-wide church.

Empire builders, who have sought to make physical empires by military might, have done great harm, but Christians ought to have "empires in their minds," not empires of physical dominion, but the world-wide dominion of a kingdom which is not of this world, the kingdom of God, the kingdom of righteousness and peace.

May we hasten to carry the good news of the gospel into all the world, in every way possible. Amen.

Internal Environment

Week 53—Day 1   **Read Ps. 20**

A famous chemist, Claude Bernard, wrote much about what he called man's "internal environment." He meant that man and other higher organisms are self-contained systems somewhat like refrigerators, unaffected by most external changes. In man's mind and heart there is also an internal environment. We can have an "interior climate" of trust and devotion when the outside weather of surroundings is cold and difficult. Here is the report of a man who had his own spiritual "inward environment." He said, "Yea, though I walk through the valley of the shadow of death, I will fear no evil, for thou art with me."

Help us to face life with a heart full of courage because we put our trust in thee, O Lord. Amen.